LEADING Cross-Culturally

Covenant Relationships for Effective Christian Leadership

Sherwood G. LINGENFELTER

Baker Academic

a division of Baker Publishing Group

Grand Rapids, Michigan

© 2008 by Sherwood G. Lingenfelter

Published by Baker Academic
a division of Baker Publishing Group
P.O. Box 6287, Grand Rapids, MI 49516-6287
www.bakeracademic.com

Printed in the United States of America

Library of Congress Cataloging-in-Publication Data
Lingenfelter, Sherwood G.
    Leading cross-culturally : covenant relationships for effective Christian leadership / Sherwood G. Lingenfelter.
       p.   cm.
   Includes bibliographical references (p.   ) and index.
   ISBN 978-0-8010-3605-7 (pbk.)
    1. Christian leadership. 2. Intercultural communication—Religious aspects—Christianity. I. Title.
   BV652.1.L57 2008
   253—dc22   2008018660

10   11   12   13   14   15   16   8   7   6   5   4   3   2

Dedicated to my father

Galen M. Lingenfelter

who loved God and God's people,
who modeled and mentored the Christ-centered
disciplines of obedience, weakness, and forgiveness,
and who empowered me to exercise my gifts of study,
teaching, and preaching when I was sixteen.

Contents

Preface

This book is the third in a series that addresses the issues of culture and the practice of cross-cultural ministry. The first book, *Ministering Cross-Culturally*, was written for people called to serve and witness for Jesus Christ in any culture other than their own. Developing a framework of contrasting values, the book guides the reader to begin by understanding one's values as a culture-bearing person, then to understand the contrasting values of others, and ultimately to learn how to add to one's cultural repertoire to be effective in cross-cultural ministry. Looking to the incarnation of Jesus into our human world as a metaphor for our ministries, the book challenges the reader to enter another culture, learn its language and customs, adapt to its values and structures, and live incarnationally in that context to bear witness to Jesus Christ.

The second book, *Teaching Cross-Culturally*, was written by my wife, Judith, and me for the Western-trained educator who is working or planning to work in a non-Western schooling setting or in the multicultural schools and universities in the major cities of North America. The goal of this work is to help teachers to understand their personal culture of teaching and learning, and then to equip the reader to become an effective learner in another cultural context, with specific focus on learning for teaching. By reflecting on the cultural differences and conflicts we have with others from the perspectives of Scripture and our faith in Jesus Christ, we show how the Bible gives us principles for living that transcend culture, but we often miss appropriate application of those principles because of our cultural blindness. We therefore seek to discern where we are culturally blind and then learn how to cope with that blindness in our teaching and other cross-cultural relationships.

The intended audience for *Leading Cross-Culturally* is broader than that for the first two books, for it speaks to Western and non-Western leaders who are working or planning to work with and lead people in multicultural teams and ministry contexts. Significant attention is given to issues of cultural diversity and ministry partnerships that cross cultural boundaries, and to the way that cultural biases of every kind create obstacles to effective leadership and ministry partnerships. But more importantly, the topic of leadership cannot be addressed biblically without engaging universal issues of control and power and the human interests and emotions that arise from our struggles over them. Given that focus on power, which pervades all cultural expressions of leadership, the book is relevant to anyone leading or preparing to lead in church and mission contexts.

Whatever the leadership assignment—a short-term ministry outreach, a multicultural ministry team, a local church, or a parachurch mission organization—the cultural issues and power obstacles to effective leadership are common to all. I therefore have several goals for this book. The first goal is to help leaders to understand their personal culture of leadership, and how that culture pervades their thinking about vision, community, and teamwork. We all participate in social and cultural contexts that become the norm for our expectations and behavior toward others. Unless we have a clear understanding of self and our own culture, and how its beliefs and values restrict our acceptance and service of others, we will not readily reach an understanding of others or be able to serve them effectively. I challenge readers to examine their culturally bound vision, values, and rewards in light of Jesus's teaching about and practice of the kingdom of God.

The second goal is to equip the reader to become an effective learner in another cultural context, with specific focus on learning to build communities of trust. Toward that end, we will examine in depth the relationship of culture to leading, to following, and to building effective ministry teams. Leadership is always part of a larger community context, and for multicultural teams, members bring varied context assumptions to both leading and following. The most difficult challenge is to build teams and communities whose members trust one another. My objectives in this exploration are to show how our "default cultures" undermine the trust essential to effective teamwork, and to help leaders grasp, apply, and train others to obey the teachings of Scripture that are essential to the transformation of teams into covenant missional communities.

The third goal is to reflect on how the human propensity to seek power and control pervades all persons and cultures and infects leaders of every kind. Through a careful analysis of power and power-seeking behavior in leaders, the book examines the temptations that leaders face in all cultural settings, temptations that undermine the work of Christian disciples everywhere to follow Christ. The book illustrates how these temptations, and our human failure to obey Christ when tempted, undermine ministry effectiveness in every corner of the world.

The fourth and most challenging goal is to define the pathways for biblically based, Christ-centered, power-giving leadership in single-culture and multicultural contexts. I will reaffirm that the Bible gives us principles for living that transcend both our human sinfulness and the prison of our culture, but we often fail to apply those principles appropriately because of our selfish motivations and interests and our cultural blindness. This book explores how both our personal brokenness and our cultural blindness create obstacles to obedience and effective leadership, and then illustrates how, through the grace of God, many have overcome both brokenness and blindness to become very effective, power-giving leaders in any cultural context.

The ultimate goal is to give joyful service as servants of the Master, inviting others to follow Christ as we follow Christ. Everyone called to ministry wants to experience God's blessing, the fruitfulness of the Spirit, and the joy of seeing others follow and discover new, abundant life in Christ. Achieving this goal is most challenging when we come together in multicultural teams—bringing old identities, habits, and expectations to the challenge of working together for the mission of God. By exposing the pitfalls of disobedience common to ministry teams and then uncovering pathways to obedience, I pray that the Holy Spirit will use this work to help those he has anointed for service to exercise power-giving leadership that mobilizes others for ministry. To this end, I have provided practical illustrations and aids from ministries around the world.

During the past thirty years, I have worked with many colleagues who are leading in multicultural contexts. Some have received cross-cultural training, but that training has rarely included any specific guidance on leadership. I have found that people commonly assume that leadership is the same everywhere, and that they have been trained adequately to guide others. This book provides many case studies that illustrate the often disastrous consequences of leading from these false assumptions.

I am indebted to many friends and colleagues for the case studies in this book and for their numerous insights as we have dialogued together about the challenges of leading cross-culturally. I owe a special debt of thanks to my friends Louis Shanks, Harriet Hill, Jim and Ginny Tomlinson, John Watters, and many others in Wycliffe International; to Harald Gorges, Detlef Krause, and Manuel and Mihamm Rauchholz in the Liebenzell Mission in Germany; to church leaders Nobumasa Mitsuhashi and Akira Izuta of RENGO in Japan; and to Chul Shin Lee, Timothy Kiho Park, and other church and university leaders in Korea. I am especially grateful to my former doctoral students, who have taught me so much from their research and personal ministry experience, including Lorraine Dierck at Biola University and Alan Weaver, Jin Seok Park, Christopher Flanders, and Anita Koeshall at Fuller Theological Seminary. I thank these men and women and my colleagues in ministry—Doug McConnell, Paul Rhoads, Peter Lin, and Gilles Gravelle—who gave significant time to reading this manuscript and helped me correct errors and clarify and sharpen earlier drafts. I am also grateful to Jim Kinney and the very fine editorial staff at Baker Academic for their continuing confidence in and enhancement of these books.

1

What Is Leading Cross-Culturally?

Church Planting and the Internet Café: A Case Study

Galen and Kate graduated from Midwest Bible Seminary in the United States, where God gave them a vision for multiplication church planting in Eurasia. Henry, a Chinese from Singapore, caught his passion for mission while preparing for ministry in Singapore and married Myra, a Filipina accountant who attended his local church. They joined an international mission where they met Galen and Kate, and together they decided to form a church-planting team to work in Eurasia.

After spending a year in language school together, they moved to a large city in Eurasia where they began their ministry. Henry, gifted in evangelism, had soon gathered together a group of young people who wanted to know more about Jesus. Myra, with her gift of hospitality, and Kate, with her gifts of evangelism and music, made these gatherings great fun and fellowship. Within months Kate had led several young women to pray to receive Christ, and Henry had led three young men. As Henry continued evangelistic outreach, Galen began to teach the men the foundational doctrines of the Christian faith, which he felt essential to their growth and maturity. Kate tried to encourage the women to study Scripture with her, but although they promised to come, only two or three did so regularly. Although these young people came from two different ethnic groups, the team used the national language of government and schooling for their ministry.

As the team developed more intimate friendships with these new believers, they discovered that faith in Christ came with significant costs. Several expressed fear about exclusion from their families if they should disclose their new faith. To make matters more tense, the parents of two of the young men banished them from their homes after they learned that they had become followers of Christ. Galen and Kate asked church members in the United States to help provide food and shelter for these young men during their crises. As the team struggled with how to become a positive presence in the local community, Henry proposed that they start a small business, an Internet café, where the two young men could work and make a living. Henry raised money from his home church in Singapore to purchase computers, and Galen challenged his home church to lease a shop in the market area where they could open the café. Within a few months they had an Internet café up and running, and they hired the men and women in their discipleship group to run the business. Myra, with her business background, served as the financial manager and accountant.

The café proved very appealing to urban youth and also solved several ministry problems. The men who needed support now had a regular job and could afford their own food and lodging. Several of the women also worked in the café, where Kate then held regular Bible studies to help them mature in their faith. For the next three years, the café business created many new contacts, and Henry and Kate guided the local believers working there to lead many local youth to make decisions for Christ. The fellowship grew to nearly thirty who attended weekend worship services in Galen's rented house. The role of the missionaries, however, had become more complex as they now provided access to financial as well as spiritual benefits.

From the time he had gained his vision for church planting in seminary, Galen had as his goal to turn over as quickly as possible the responsibilities of the church plant to local leaders. In the fourth year of this ministry Galen and Henry decided, after a season of prayer and fasting, that the men they had discipled were ready to begin to assume leadership of this blooming church plant. After assessing the spiritual gifts of the men and women in the group, they gradually encouraged individuals with the appropriate gifts to take leadership responsibility. With the help of Kate and Myra, they encouraged men and women alike to lead worship and to teach, and they rotated the responsibility for preaching among the men. While these young people did the work, Galen observed that men and women alike continued to come to them for direction. Further, once or twice a month Galen had to step in at the last minute and preach, when the man assigned for that week called to say he was sick and could not come. Kate also found herself helping more than she wanted to in the weekly Bible studies, as these young women turned to her for guidance and then stepped back as she responded to questions and issues of discussion.

Over the next two years, Galen and Henry turned the weekly services over to three of the young national leaders, all of whom worked in the Internet café. One had become the supervisor of the café and was quite effective in business. However, this man was not an effective preacher, and the people began to complain about him. Some in the group, seeing the pattern of other church plants in the area, asked that Galen and Henry appoint just one person to be the preaching pastor of the church. When Galen took a stand against this, the man who wanted to be preaching pastor left the group, and fifteen others from his ethnic group went with him to form their own fellowship. Three of the women who left still worked in the Internet café, and this created problems for their supervisor, who was hurt by their rejection of him as a spiritual leader.

When Galen and Kate departed for their second furlough, they were deeply discouraged. What had been such a promising church plant seemed shattered. Their vision had been to equip men and women to share Christ with others and to become the leaders of a new church-planting movement. Many young people had responded to the gospel, and they had seemed ripe for discipleship and leadership training. Yet, somehow the momentum had been lost. The fellowship was broken, relationships were shattered over who should preach, and instead of a movement, these believers wanted a traditional church structure that focused on Sunday services and preaching rather than mission. The only thing that seemed to be working was the Internet café, and in that Myra, as the financial manager and accountant, assured its ongoing success.

Good People, Misguided Leadership

In the example of the Internet café, we can discern a fundamental flaw in this team's leadership. Although Galen and Henry thought they had done an effective job of church planting, after nearly eight years of work they had become the owners of the business, senior management that propped up all the ministries. Everything that happened originated from their vision and initiative. Although they had carefully nurtured a team of three men, Galen notes that these men turned to them for direction in even minor matters. The church they had planted looked very much like a successful community of believers, but in reality these people had become dependent on the expatriate missionaries.

What went wrong? These missionaries had learned the national language of government and education. They had diligently shared the gospel with people who had not heard, and when many responded, they organized them as a community of believers and faithfully taught them the foundational doctrines and practices of Christian living and witness. With their considerable ministry training and skills, they had organized a form of church that they believed would reproduce and tried diligently to train local people to carry out these ministries. In spite of their best efforts, their leadership training failed to achieve their objectives. At times these new believers deferred to expatriate skill and expertise, and at other times they resorted to familiar local patterns of leadership.

Although Galen and Henry were frustrated with their disciples' responses, they did not recognize their contribution to the situation. What they had hoped would become a movement of their disciples sharing Christ in their communities and beyond was instead a weak community propped up by the skill and diligent work of these two missionary couples. In spite of their theological and missionary training, in the stress of an emerging church-planting ministry, Galen, Kate, Henry, and Myra had defaulted to habits of leadership and church from their home cultures and had failed to understand that their disciples were doing the same.

This book is about very good people who practice misguided leadership, leadership that seems right but jeopardizes and sometimes destroys their vision and ministries. Like Galen, Kate, Henry, and Myra, most of these people feel called by God and sacrifice themselves wholeheartedly to the work of ministry. Many are deeply sensitive to the people they lead to Christ and desire above everything else to see these women and men mature in their relationship with Christ and become part of the work of ministry to reach their communities with the gospel. Yet all Christian leaders, regardless of their cultural background, carry their personal histories and cultural biases with them wherever they serve. And like Galen and Henry, they cannot see how their histories and culture shape their ministries and blind them to the unintended consequences of these practices and values in their discipleship and leadership-training activities. They in fact are locked into "traditional behavior," derived from their life histories and social context, even though young people such as Galen often adamantly deny having any "traditions" that influence their ministry.

But the fact is that all people engaged in Christian ministry bring to their work a culture and tradition of ministry and leadership. Throughout the history of the church, Christian communities have developed many and diverse understandings of what constitutes leading and leadership. In their recent edited volume, Richard Mouw and Eric Jacobsen (2006) present nine different traditions of leadership in the faith communities of Western culture. Each of them presumes certain characteristics of structure, certain notions about authority, and an understanding of theology and faith that influences and defines what each tradition means by leading and leadership. And each of these cases documents in some way a struggle with the inherent contradictions between social traditions and the teachings of Scripture on faith community and leadership.

The argument presented in the following chapters examines how even the most current traditions of leadership are culturally bound, and when applied in cross-cultural and multicultural contexts, these traditions become obstacles to effective ministry.

What Is Leading?

Robert Banks and Bernice Ledbetter (2004) have done a masterful job of summarizing the vast literature on leadership written in the United States. In the opening chapter of their book, they address the question of the difference between leadership and management. They state very clearly that management is not leadership. "Leadership activity is aligning people" by translating vision and values "into understandable and attainable acts. . . . Managers achieve their goals by organizing and staffing" (2004, 18). Banks and Ledbetter go on to define the characteristics of leadership in terms of vision, setting direction, monitoring trends, and motivating and inspiring people to follow. Their insights are helpful as we seek to answer the question, what is leading? Yet secular and business perspectives on leadership are inadequate for Christian ministry.

For the purpose of this book, I will reference the leadership literature from time to time but give priority and privilege to insights that we gain from the life and teaching of Jesus and from the Scriptures written by those who followed him. This book is about the clash of worldviews inherent in cross-cultural and multicultural relationships and the impact of that clash on the practice of leadership. In my view the gospel is transcultural, and the life and teaching of Jesus gives Christian leaders the spiritual resources essential to meet the challenges of interpersonal conflicts and misunderstandings that arise when teams and followers embrace conflicting worldviews. The Internet café church-planting team thought they were applying these spiritual resources well, but they failed to acknowledge and address the worldview conflicts.

The language and definitions of leading that follow have been stimulated by the leadership literature and study and reflection on the Gospels and Epistles of the New Testament. The discussion focuses on issues of relationships and community that are foundational to the life and work of Christian community. I begin by defining several key features of what constitutes leading and then conclude with a statement of what "leading" means as addressed in this book.

The first characteristic of leading is *building trust within a relational community*. Galen and Henry focused on teaching new believers the truths of Scripture and the practice of ministry, but they did not focus on building mutual trust. Likewise, Kate and Myra gave greater priority to evangelism and good business than to building trust relationships essential for leadership in Christian community. In a public, business, or secular context, it is clearly possible to lead without having trust relationships; within Christian community, however, the building of trust is a fundamental characteristic of leadership. In John's Gospel, Jesus makes it clear that the people who follow him, the "good shepherd," trust him (John 10:4–5). They know his voice. They will not follow a stranger because they do not recognize the stranger's voice. From the perspective of the Gospels, building trust is a key feature of leading. Many stories illustrate how Jesus engaged in those trust-building relationships with his disciples. John 1:35–51 describes how Jesus encountered Andrew and a friend and invited them to come and stay with him. They followed him and spent a Sabbath with him. Afterward Andrew invited his brother Simon Peter to come and get acquainted with Jesus. Through these relational engagements, Jesus inspired the confidence and trust of these men.

The second characteristic of leading in the life of Christ is the *defining of a compelling vision* for life. Andrew reported to his brother Simon, "We have found the Messiah." Jesus then encountered Peter and Andrew fishing, and he challenged them, "'Come, follow me, . . . and I will send you out to catch people.' At once they left their nets and followed him" (Matt. 4:19–20). Jesus proclaimed a new vision of the kingdom of heaven that redefined the kind of relationships that people have with one another and with God. "Blessed are the poor in spirit, for theirs is the kingdom of heaven. . . . Blessed are the merciful, for they will be shown mercy. . . . Blessed are the peacemakers, for they will be called the children of God" (Matt. 5:3–9). To reflect again on the case study, Galen and Kate were driven by a vision for multiplication church planting, but this vision had little if any meaning for their new converts and disciples. Further, none of these new believers understood the wonder of the kingdom of heaven, and none was willing to leave everything and follow (Matt. 19:27).

A third characteristic of leading is *stepping out ahead*. Again in the Gospel of John, Jesus says, "When he has brought out all his own, he goes on ahead of them, and his sheep follow him because they know his voice" (John 10:4). Jesus did not ask his disciples to do anything that he had not already done with them. He called them to accompany him as he proclaimed the good news of the kingdom, taught the crowds, and healed the sick. After they had seen and heard him many times, he sent them out, two by two, to do the same. Jesus's example suggests that leading means doing the things that you expect those who follow you to do and showing them by your actions and example that this is the way to walk and to live. Our Eurasian church planters understood this principle and did lead by action and example. But once again they did not grasp the worldview conflicts, and they quickly reverted to the routines of their home culture—singing, preaching, teaching, study, and then the business of the Internet café. These activities, perhaps church work rather than kingdom work, proved to be the undoing of their vision.

The fourth principle that Jesus employed was *calling others to follow* him. Jesus met Peter, James, and John at their fishing boats, overwhelmed them with a catch that nearly caused their boats to sink, and then called them to leave it all and follow him (Luke 5:1–11). Jesus also encountered Levi, a tax collector, and invited him to follow. The importance of the principle of "calling" is that people often are waiting for such an invitation, and when they receive it, they respond by following. Paul encourages Corinthian believers: "Follow my example, as I follow the example of Christ" (1 Cor. 11:1). Following Christ must be the first priority of every believer, and that means becoming a follower before one even considers a calling to lead. Galen and Myra were particularly good at inviting others to follow, but they were too good at what they did. Their followers were intimidated, fearing their lack of skill and confidence. Galen's disciples deferred to his preaching and teaching skill, and Myra's employees were just that. None of these local people felt secure enough to step up and participate as leaders in this new context.

The fifth and last principle is *empowering those who follow* you—a leader or leadership team (two or more)—and sending them out to do the same things that you have done. Luke 9:1–6 details how Jesus granted power and authority to the Twelve who had followed him and sent them out to proclaim the kingdom of God. From this example, we see that leading is much more than having people follow you; it is mentoring them in such a way that you can empower and release them to do the same thing on their own that you have done with them. The men and women in the Eurasia team sought to mentor new believers, but they did this from their own cultural experience and agendas. They failed to learn how mentors lead others in this Eurasian culture and rejected essential social activities and expectations that would have enabled trust and the empowerment of others.

Leading, then, is inspiring people who participate with you in a community of trust to follow you—a leader or a leadership team—and be empowered by you to achieve a compelling vision of faith. Working from this definition, and the example of Jesus from the Gospels, we might ask Galen and his team to reflect on their church plant. How did they end up becoming an "Internet café" that propped up a weak church plant? As we reflect on their story, we see that they clearly had a vision for church planting and training leaders to lead this new church. They excelled in stepping out ahead, showing what must be done, and gaining the trust of their disciples to follow them; in fact, the disciples themselves often limited their behavior to following. But as we look more closely at Galen and Henry's plan, their priority was "the organization and establishing of a new church." Galen and his team called the meeting and identified the men and women who should become the core leaders. Galen, Kate, Henry, and Myra set the agenda and the time frame in which all these things should happen. And Galen had as his goal "to turn over as quickly as possible the responsibilities of the church plant to local leaders." Although Henry's Chinese background made him less urgent, he too wanted his disciples to take more responsibilities.

Galen and his team failed in the most important priority for leaders: building a community of trust. These believers trusted Galen and the mission team, but they did not trust one another, an obstacle exacerbated by their two different ethnic backgrounds. When Galen suggested that they take responsibility for preaching and other duties, fear of rejection by their peers paralyzed them. These believers accepted the formal organization proposed by the missionaries as long as the missionaries took responsibility. When Galen proposed that they step into these roles, they did not trust one another or the Lord enough to risk failure.

The data in the case also suggest that these believers did not share the vision that motivated the mission team. They did not see themselves as part of a church-planting team. They did not envision the possibility of being like Galen and Henry or Kate and Myra, doing the things that these expatriates did. And although the team tried to push them into these roles, every time one new believer or the other did the work of ministry, they only went as far as they felt comfortable. Galen and Kate often stepped in to assist, and Myra managed the café finances alone. Galen and Kate tried to empower their disciples to lead, but they left for furlough in despair over the fragmentation of this ministry. All four of these missionaries failed to understand the culture and values of these Eurasian people groups, and they did not learn how to engage their disciples in such a way that empowerment would be possible.

What Is Leading Cross-Culturally?

The complexity of leading cross-culturally lies in the challenge of building a community of trust among people who come from two or more cultural traditions that provoke a clash of worldviews. Because people rely on their cultural understandings for meaning, security, and significance, cultural differences have inherent power in human relationships to foster fear and mistrust. Cultural values related to such simple matters as how one deals with time, crises, and achievement can precipitate serious conflicts when people cling to diverging expectations. When people disagree about deeper values, such as those regarding one's relationship to God, ancestors, or community, or those of satisfying personal and corporate interests, the gulf of mistrust may become so wide that working together becomes impossible.

Also, different cultures inevitably have different structures and processes for organizing community relationships and work. When culturally diverse people try to work together toward mutual goals, their assumptions about structure and working relationships may create serious issues of conflict and disagreement. Unless people resolve these differences, they cannot work together effectively. Further, each cultural community has its socially defined understandings about how issues of resources and power should be managed. Some communities insist on sharing resources and upholding power as a collective group. Others delegate or allocate the management of resources and power to an individual or an organizational hierarchy within the community. Such differences about how to structure control of resources, power, and authority always create problems in work requiring trust and cooperation.

Finally, every community has its own standards of accountability, and the issues and structures of accountability vary significantly across cultures. Some societies, and particularly Western industrial nations, insist on accountability structures that require extensive documentation and external structures and processes. Others insist on accountability as a product of relationships and emphasize that people are accountable primarily to the groups to which they belong and to the standards the groups hold for their members. As a consequence, building a community of trust is always a major challenge for cross-cultural leadership.

Leading cross-culturally, then, is inspiring people who come from two or more cultural traditions to participate with you (the leader or leadership team) in building a community of trust and then to follow you and be empowered by you to achieve a compelling vision of faith.

Why Is Leading So Difficult?

On July 1, 2007, I began my twentieth year of academic leadership, first as provost and senior vice president at Biola University, then as dean of the School of World Mission at Fuller Theological Seminary, and now as provost and senior vice president at Fuller. Over these nearly two decades of leadership, I have found that leading is always an incredibly difficult challenge. One might attribute that to my personal limitations and character, but as I examine the tenure record of pastors, academic leaders, and mission leaders, my experience is not unique. The average term of a president of a college or university in the United States is less than seven years. George Barna reports (www.barna.org) that the average pastor in the United States serves only five years. Research on the tenure of senior pastors suggests that senior pastors stay in such positions fewer than eight years. One wonders why leadership is so challenging that people choose not to continue to serve in leadership positions.

I personally have found that it is much more difficult to play the game of leadership than to teach or write about it. I began doing research on leadership as part of my doctoral dissertation work in 1969. Since that time I have done considerable research, writing, and teaching on this topic. I find it relatively easy to develop lectures on leadership out of my research and to give students the principles that I have learned from that research regarding how to practice effective leadership. Writing this book has been much easier than leading in any of the contexts in which I have lived and worked.

Why is leading so difficult? In the summer of 2007, the news media gave considerable attention to the fact that the Philadelphia Phillies had lost more games in their professional history than any other professional sports team. Sports commentators cited the ten thousand losses of the Phillies as a national landmark of team and leadership failure. The challenging fact is that most professional teams lose more games than they win, and most leaders fail to provide effective leadership for their teams and organizations more often than they succeed. The hard facts are that leading is a very difficult thing to do, and the challenges of leadership usually result in something less than the success to which leaders aspire. Perhaps this is a key reason why we see leadership turnover in the church, the university, and government. Leading is simply a very difficult and challenging task.

Facing Weakness and Dependence

In my personal experience as a leader, I have come to understand that my weaknesses significantly affect my leadership. I have observed, however, that my weaknesses are closely correlated with my strengths. When I rely on my talents, I tend to place my trust in myself rather than in God. As a consequence, my strength becomes one of my most serious weaknesses.

I also have areas of blindness and weakness in my working relationships with people. I have learned over the years that if I do not depend on other people in the body of Christ to help me in those areas—if I ignore these weaknesses or try to rely on my strengths—there are critical defects in my leadership. I cannot lead effectively without the diverse gifts of others in the body of Christ. My assistants in my work as provost have been some of the most important people in my life. They help me see what other people need when I don't recognize this. They coax me to do thoughtful things, such as writing birthday cards and sending thank-you notes, when my natural disposition inclines me not to give those things priority. My priorities, felt needs, understanding, and skills—as gifted or as limited as they might be—are inadequate for the challenges that I face in trying to lead a diverse community of people. I am capable of leading at a place like Fuller only when I am surrounded by people with diverse talents and gifts who can complement, correct, and expand the talents and spiritual gifts that God has given me.

In brief, I have come to understand that I am completely dependent on God's people around me, people who have diverse gifts and are capable of contributing, adding value, critiquing, and expanding the competencies and gifts that the Lord has given to me. Some of my most significant failures as a leader have come when I have ignored my dependence on others and the limitations of the gifts that God has given me.

The temptations that I most often face bubble out of the emotional cauldron of my personal strengths and weaknesses: being impatient with God's people, oftentimes expecting them to do things my way on a schedule and calendar that fits my expectations, and focusing on results. Although I pray often for the Lord to clothe me with compassion, kindness, humility, gentleness, and patience, I find myself significantly lacking in all those virtues. Instead of showing compassion toward coworkers, I too often judge their motives and respond to their performance with impatience and criticism. Even though I know this is not God's plan for us, the temptations ferment daily, and I find myself judging, condemning, and being impatient.

One of the most subtle and destructive temptations for leaders is arrogance. Early in my tenure as provost at Biola University, a position of authority in which I was affirmed by many around me for my work, I soon began to think more highly of myself than I should have. Working with a large team of colleagues in a supervisory role, I was routinely called upon to evaluate performance. I found myself judging rather than providing constructive counsel, and, impatient with the performance of some, I yielded to arrogance. Arrogance is a deception about self and others, and the community often does not help to counter it. For example, people at Biola and at Fuller referred to me as "provost" instead of using my name, and they treated me as if I had elevated importance, which encouraged me to be the arrogant person that I was inclined to become. Yielding to the temptation of arrogance has a devastating impact. As soon as I think I am important, I begin to look down on others who are part of the body, and the inflated sense of self becomes a source of personal and leadership disaster.

A second common temptation is seeking to control and exercise power in order to accomplish one's will and achieve desired results. Yielding to the temptation to control and forcibly influence outcomes completely undermines and destroys spiritual ministry. We cannot do the work of the kingdom of God by exercising the tools of the devil. When we distort God's will, when we seek power to achieve the ends that seem right to us, when we refuse to love as Christ commanded us, when we use power to make things happen that we think are essential, we have fallen into the trap that the evil one so cleverly sets for us, and we destroy the work of the kingdom of God.

A third area of temptation lies in what I have come to experience as "the silent God." Often in my journey I have cried out to the Lord in anguish about some of the circumstances that I have faced in my leadership. More times than not, God was silent. I did not hear a voice or find a particular verse of Scripture that gave me assurance or direction; instead, I experienced God as silent. As I reflect on this, I interpret it not as the absence of God but rather as part of the mystery of God's relationship with human beings. God's revelation of self comes first in the Scriptures, and as Jesus recounted in the story of the rich man and Lazarus, God's voice in the Scriptures is enough. We have the Scriptures to guide us, to provide wise counsel, and to give us direction for leadership. I know these Scriptures, have studied and memorized them, and I come back to them time and again. Perhaps God is silent because God has already spoken through the Scriptures and is waiting for me to respond and to obey what I have heard.

However, in the anxiety that comes with the work of leadership, not knowing where to turn or what to do, seeking guidance and receiving contradictory counsel from different directions, I have doubted God. I have doubted God's presence and direction, and I have questioned why leading should be so painful and people so difficult. At times I have been moved to desperation, wondering if God had heard, or had an interest in responding, and if there would be an end to the pain that I was experiencing. I can now say with assurance that God will often be silent, that I will not receive supernatural direction for every crisis that I face, and that I will be challenged to trust God to the extent that God has chosen to reveal God's will and purpose in the Scriptures. Sometimes I feel the presence and even the direction of the Holy Spirit, but those are unusual times. Most of the time I must act in each given circumstance based on what I understand to be obedience to the Word of God given to me in the Scriptures.

Marguerite Shuster, in her classic work on our obsession with power in human life, points to the way of weakness, fellowship, and forgiveness (1987, 209–34). Shuster argues that only by following Jesus and understanding that the path of effectiveness is through weakness are we able to achieve the will of the Master. Jesus challenges us to follow him and to understand that we are weak; only as we depend on him within the supportive fellowship of Christian community can we have the power to accomplish his purpose. Jesus also reminds us of the essential importance of fellowship and forgiveness in our relationships with others. We cannot accomplish the work of the kingdom of God unless we are willing to work together in the fellowship of a loving community and forgive as he has forgiven us. Paul reminds us of this in Colossians 3:15, and Jesus emphasizes it repeatedly in the Gospels. In our relationships in covenant community, we are to forgive even as Jesus has forgiven us.

In the pages that follow, we will examine many other case studies and reflect on the question, why is leading so difficult? What are the challenges that keep us from fulfilling our vision and aspirations as God's servants, to lead cross-cultural or multicultural teams, extending God's healing reign in our broken world? Chapters 2 and 3 focus on the question of how we inspire people to achieve a compelling vision of faith. How does God call and then motivate people to follow and work as one body for the mission of God? What is kingdom work, what are the essential kingdom values for partnership in kingdom work, and what should we expect as rewards for kingdom work?

Chapters 4 through 7 explore the leadership challenge of building a community of trust when people come from different cultural traditions. Anyone who aspires to lead a multicultural team must invest time and resources to learn who the people on the team are, what expectations they have about teamwork, and how those expectations create the potential for mistrust and conflict. Leaders must understand that individuals in stressful situations, despite their considerable cross-cultural learning and experience, regress to their default culture— habits, values, and patterns of interaction acquired in childhood. When members of a multicultural team are so distressed that they begin to operate in these default modes, the dysfunction and failure of the team is virtually assured. How can leaders help team members break the habits of their default culture? What priority should a leader give to the creation of a covenant community in which team members commit first to one another as people of God and then to working together as one on the mission of God?

Chapters 8 through 11 develop the concept of power-giving leadership and define pathways to empower others to achieve a compelling vision of faith. Beginning with the proposition that all people are inherently "power seekers," we examine the implication for leaders that team relationships will be fraught with struggles for power and control. What then does Scripture teach about our exercise of will and desire to control others and outcomes? Drawing a contrast between mentoring to manage and mentoring to lead, we ask why leaders should take the risk of releasing control to emerging leaders.

Finally, chapters 12 and 13 reflect upon the challenges of leading cross-culturally by reviewing case studies from earlier chapters in light of the responsibility and challenge every leader faces when exercising power associated with his or her social and spiritual authority. One cannot lead without exercising the power inherent in all social and team relationships. The challenge for a leader is to understand how power is abused in every social environment, and to learn how to use power biblically in different social structures. But most importantly, leaders must learn how to align people with their diverse gifts to achieve the vision that God has given them and then empower them to be about this kingdom work.

Part 1

Inspiring People

2

Kingdom Vision and Work

Whose Vision for India? A Case Study

As I tried to look ahead, my spirit suggested a vision to plant 1,000 churches in a period of 10 years. This seemed like a goal we could achieve! With a good effort we should be able to accomplish the vision! Then I shared the vision with some of my friends. A pastor from a Methodist church told me, "Bobby, do you know that we, the Methodist church in India, have been in existence for over a hundred years and our church movement has not planted 100 churches? You must be crazy to think you will be able to plant 1,000 churches in ten years."

After this strong negative reaction, I was embarrassed! Feeling like a fool to make such a statement, I really got angry with God. I was certain that the Holy Spirit had prompted me to envision 1,000 churches and if He had not done this, I would not have become the subject of public ridicule.

In my private debate with the Lord, God humbled me when the Holy Spirit said, "Bobby, you are not going to plant a single church. You see I am going to build my church. You are only going to be my instrument." After hearing this from the Lord, I was soon back on the road sharing this vision and inviting people to join me in this work. . . .

No sooner was I back on the road sharing the vision for 1,000 churches than God began to help me see the bigger picture. Suddenly, I realized my strategy would never fulfill the vision God had placed in my heart. India's people inhabited more than 600,000 villages, and I heard the Holy Spirit ask, "What will 1,000 churches do to reach the nation of India?"

I did not want to think about those numbers. Many people already thought I was crazy to think we could plant 1,000 churches in ten years. At first I said, "I am not going to discuss this, please find someone else." Then I begged the Lord to leave me alone as my task was large enough. I reminded the Lord that people were already laughing at me—they might throw me into a mental hospital and declare me insane.

In spite of all my excuses the Holy Spirit patiently prodded me about my vision. Finally, I decided to negotiate with the Lord. Remembering that HBI [Hindustan Bible Institute] had graduated over 1,000 men and women, I imagined that we could invite them to join us in the vision and ask each to each plant 100 churches, so that we would have 100,000 churches. This seemed much closer to the need and I hoped the Holy Spirit would be satisfied. (Gupta and Lingenfelter 2006, 105–6)

Leading cross-culturally is *inspiring people* who come from two or more cultural traditions to participate with you in building a community of trust and then to follow you and be empowered by you *to achieve a compelling vision of faith*. In the case study above, Bobby Gupta describes his struggle with the Lord about a vision for the evangelization of India. He candidly exposes his debate with the Holy Spirit and with the people of God in his network of relationships. He must ask the questions: Is this my vision or God's? How will I know? How much of this vision flows from my experience and relationships? How much flows from Scripture? How is God speaking in personal and corporate prayer? How is God moving in others to confirm that the vision is more than me? What does Scripture teach us about kingdom vision and kingdom work? If we hope to lead cross-culturally, we must search for answers to these questions.

What Is Kingdom Vision?

Jesus returned to Galilee in the power of the Spirit, and news about him spread throughout the whole countryside. He was teaching in their synagogues, and everyone praised him.

He went to Nazareth, where he had been brought up, and on the Sabbath day he went into the synagogue, as was his custom. He stood up to read, and the scroll of the prophet Isaiah was handed to him. Unrolling it, he found the place where it is written:

> "The Spirit of the Lord is on me,
>   because he has anointed me
>   to proclaim good news to the poor.
> He has sent me to proclaim freedom for the prisoners
>   and recovery of sight for the blind,
> to release the oppressed,
>   to proclaim the year of the Lord's favor."

Then he rolled up the scroll, gave it back to the attendant and sat down. The eyes of everyone in the synagogue were fastened on him. He began by saying to them, "Today this scripture is fulfilled in your hearing." . . .

Then he went down to Capernaum, a town in Galilee, and on the Sabbath he taught the people. They were amazed at his teaching, because his words had authority. (Luke 4:14–21, 31–32)

The vision essential for cross-cultural leadership is based on an understanding of what the Scriptures teach of the kingdom of God and the vision that flows out of the power of the Holy Spirit to establish that kingdom now and in the ages to come. The Isaiah text, read by Jesus in his hometown, proclaims freedom for prisoners, sight for the blind, and release from oppression. Jesus declares that God has sent him on this day to fulfill this prophetic vision. In the context of Roman occupation, freedom for prisoners and relief from oppression were certainly germane to the community life. Many other texts speak of the multitudes suffering from sickness, blindness, crippled limbs, and other physical maladies. Jesus announces that on this day, the Lord has looked with favor on this community and on his people throughout the country.

The Gospel of Matthew articulates the vision in a parallel but distinctive way:

> Jesus went throughout Galilee, teaching in their synagogues, proclaiming the good news of the kingdom, and healing every disease and sickness among the people. News about him spread all over Syria. . . .

Now when Jesus saw the crowds, he went up on a mountainside and sat
down. His disciples came to him, and he began to teach them, saying:
"Blessed are the poor in spirit,
for theirs is the kingdom of heaven." (Matt. 4:23–5:3)

The Matthew text also reports how four fishermen caught the vision
and immediately left their work and followed Jesus (Matt. 4:18–20).
That is the essence of a compelling vision for leadership. When a
leader has a vision from the Spirit of God and shares that vision with
people whom God has touched, they together leave homes, families,
and possessions to fulfill the mission of God.

In contemporary society, there are vast numbers of leaders with vision. These visions are often for very good and positive things. Most
business corporations run on the basis of a vision articulated by their
leaders on how the corporation can become a great and lasting company.
The communities of universities and theological seminaries expect their
presidents to define a vision that motivates the community to follow.
To have effective, compelling vision for ministry, the kind of vision that
will motivate people to follow, the Christian leader must have a deep
and intimate walk with Christ and listen to and be filled with the Holy
Spirit. But even more importantly, this vision must be tested in the community of the body of Christ, refined by the participation of the body
in shaping it, and then mobilized by the body in prayer and action.

In the case that opens the chapter, Bobby Gupta tells how God moved
him with compassion for the multitudes of India who had never heard of
Jesus Christ. Praying, reading Scripture, and listening to the Holy Spirit,
he sensed the Holy Spirit saying, "What will one thousand churches do to
reach the nation of India?" As Bobby continues his story, he relates how
he shared his vision to plant one hundred thousand churches in India
with a congregation in California. After the service many congratulated
him on such a great vision, but then Jim Montgomery, a member of the
congregation and founder of the movement Discipling a Whole Nation
(DAWN), quietly told him that the vision was too small. Irritated by the
challenge, Bobby said to Jim, "I know it will not meet the need, but your
goal is too high; people will not get involved." Jim replied, "Bobby, if
you begin with the wrong end in mind, you will never reach the nation."
Accepting Montgomery's challenge and offer of support, Bobby invited

a group of Indian leaders to come together in 1987 and begin a conversation about what it would take to fulfill the Great Commission in India. In that first meeting in 1987, God expanded the vision of these men to the dream of a church for every village and town, a church for every thousand people. Then God sustained them in the very challenging work of sharing vision and mobilizing people in prayer over the next decade, and through the prayer of thousands, God gave birth to an incredible church-planting movement (Gupta and Lingenfelter 2006, 106–7).

What is kingdom vision? Vision flows first from the mission of God as articulated in the Scriptures. Darrell Guder writes, "In the passion, death, and resurrection of Jesus Christ, God's salvation history reaches its climax. God's mission has arrived at its decisive point in Jesus, the Christ, the one whom God has sent. . . . The risen Lord now sends his disciples into the world to carry out the . . . mission of God that was the purpose and content of his life, death, and resurrection" (2000, 46). We are the disciples of Jesus Christ, sent out to continue the work that he began and now continues through his body, the church.

Yet it is not our task to define that mission for our time. God is already at work in the power of the Holy Spirit, and our task is to ask, how has God gone before us, and what is God already doing in our world? As we listen to the Holy Spirit and seek to align ourselves with what God is already doing in the world, God will reveal his vision and purpose for us. Gupta's story illustrates this well. God was already at work in India; the Holy Spirit had touched thousands of Hindus, revealing the presence and power of Jesus. The church was asleep, and God called Bobby, Jim, and others to awaken the church to the movement of the Holy Spirit and to call the church to prayer and obedience to follow the leading of the Holy Spirit to do God's work.

God's mission and vision requires our obedience, as we first listen to the Holy Spirit, obey by taking the first steps, and then share that vision with others, inviting them to pray and to bring others to pray. The Spirit of God motivates God's people to respond. The story of God's work in India parallels the stories told in the Gospels. In the Matthew text quoted above, we noted that Jesus went from town to town, touching people, healing them, and teaching them the good news of the kingdom of heaven. From 1987 to 2006, hundreds of Indian evangelists and pastors in hundreds of districts in India embraced the vision of a church in every village and town and proclaimed this same Jesus. They invited people to pray to Jesus, asking him to heal their sicknesses and restore their relationships. Jesus once again acted in response to their prayers—people were healed, demons cast out; people opened their hearts to Jesus and his good news, and more than two hundred thousand churches were planted (Gupta and Lingenfelter 2006, 152–55).

What Is Kingdom Work?

Once people have committed to a vision and have begun to follow a leader, they embark on the journey of kingdom work. But what is kingdom work? We do all kinds of things that constitute the essential work for us to live in human society. The essentials of working to live include procuring food and housing, sharing in exchanges with others, and striving for the well-being of the community in which one lives. These are all good and valuable things, and they are essential to human life.

I would like to distinguish between the kind of work that is essential for human existence and kingdom work. When Jesus spoke of the kingdom of heaven or the kingdom of God, he proclaimed the advent of a world in which God reached down to the poor and helpless, touching the untouchables, healing the sick and broken, and reconciling people, society, and all creation to the Creator. It is this work of the loving touch, healing, and reconciliation that I and others call "kingdom work" (Christian 1994; Linthicum 2003; Myers 2002). The Gospel of Luke relates a story that shows how Jesus conceptualized this himself.

> When Jesus had called the Twelve together, he gave them power and authority to drive out all demons and to cure diseases, and he sent them out to proclaim the kingdom of God and to heal the sick. He told them: "Take nothing for the journey—no staff, no bag, no bread, no money, no extra shirt. Whatever house you enter, stay there until you leave that town. If people do not welcome you, shake the dust off your feet when you leave their town, as a testimony against them." So they set out and went from village to village, proclaiming the good news and healing people everywhere. (Luke 9:1–6)

In this text kingdom work is "good news" and a healing touch. What is this good news? The message is that God is near and is seeking to engage humanity in a new and transforming way. As elaborated earlier in this Gospel, Jesus told his disciples to "love your enemies, do good to those who hate you" (Luke 6:27). Instead of judging and condemning, they were challenged to forgive and to be forgiven. Instead of being greedy and seeking their own interest and good, they were encouraged to give and give generously. The good news of the kingdom turns their culture upside down, challenges their values, and calls them to a deeper relationship with God and with one another. At the same time, Jesus commanded the Twelve to be a healing presence in these towns. They were not just to teach; they were to pray for those who were sick, to heal them, and to bring the power and the presence of God into the daily lives of these people.

The command that Jesus gave the Twelve is terrifying. How, even in the name of Jesus, can we heal the sick? Yet Luke states clearly that Jesus gave them power and authority to do what he sent them to do. Kingdom work is impossible without power and authority from God. We deceive ourselves if we think that we can set about this work on our own initiative. God gives power and authority only when God pleases, never at our pleading or demand. God gives only to those who follow and obey him and only in God's time and purpose. These disciples had walked with Jesus, engaged with him as he taught, cast out demons, and healed those who were sick. At the right time, Jesus sent them into the towns to do what they had observed and done with him.

So how does kingdom work apply to the challenge of leading cross-culturally? The vision is God's, the mission is God's, and the work is God's. Leading must be focused on God's good news and God's healing touch. If we aspire to work within this relationship, called by God to serve as God's messengers and hands, we can trust God to show his presence and power as we step out in faith to serve those to whom we are sent.

There are many case studies in this book of people engaged in work that they would call kingdom work. Multicultural teams in Thailand provide housing for the homeless, create income opportunities for the poor, do evangelism, equip local leaders, and minister to orphans, widows, and other people who are suffering. Others serve in the name of Christ to carry out community development, Bible translation, literacy training, and other works of benefit to people in communities that lack these basic opportunities and skills.

Kingdom work combines both good news and a healing touch. Some organizations have chosen to obey the Lord and focus only on a healing touch. Others have invested themselves wholly in the proclamation of the gospel and yet have resisted or even rejected the notion that they should provide a healing touch. Although I think that God is pleased with the obedience of both in these activities, by excluding or diminishing one part as some propose (Hesselgrave 2005, 117–38), these people have misunderstood the work he has sent us to do. A healing touch without good news or the good news without a healing touch are both incomplete expressions of the vision that Christ gave us in the Gospels. For our purposes in this book, we will talk about kingdom work as both good news and a healing touch. Tetsunao Yamamori (1993), founder of Food for the Hungry, has argued eloquently for this full-orbed commitment to the gospel. Yamamori mobilized teams for relief ministries around the world, providing food and good news for those suffering from famine and food shortages. In a similar manner, Wycliffe International has sought to provide Scriptures, literacy, and community development to assist people through a holistic ministry providing good news that transforms their total lives. Thousands of Christian ministries, from local churches to global mission organizations, have engaged in kingdom work, addressing a wide range of human concerns with good news and a healing touch. Most of these have experienced the challenges of leading cross-culturally and of mobilizing people from diverse cultures for the mission of God.

What Is the Leader's Role in Calling and Motivating?

God gives apostolic gifts to some of his people to call others to serve. This gifting is often manifest first as a deep conviction from the Holy Spirit, a sense of urgency in the soul, often provoked by a text or story from Scripture, to step out of one's normal routines of life and follow Jesus in kingdom work. God frequently gives a vision of people who have urgent and compelling needs and invites a person to take one small step of faith and obedience toward meeting those needs. When this is an apostolic gift and calling, God will show the person that the mission requires obedience to take the first step and then obedience to invite others to pray and join in this service for the Master.

John Watters, executive director of Wycliffe Bible Translators International from January 2000 to December 2007, tells the story of how the Holy Spirit moved him over a period of several months to catch a new vision for the translation of the Scriptures. As he reflects on the time when he debated whether to be a candidate for the position of international executive director, he describes how he struggled to understand what it would mean to serve in such a global role.

> At the time I was serving as Africa area director. I had heard many discussions in international meetings about what we needed to do better, what we needed to do more of, and what we needed to fix. I began to realize that a vision for the future of Bible translation could not be built on problems to be solved or issues to be addressed. A list of twelve, fifteen, or even thirty key items that needed special attention would only be a list of exhortations or therapies to pursue. Such lists are always with us. They do not constitute a vision. Such a list only calls for doing better or more of the same rather than doing differently. It can be joyless, duty bound, and focused on human effort. A vision should bring joy and a refreshment of spirit as we take on Jesus's yoke. It should lead us in dependence on God and not ourselves. It actually puts the list of problems and issues in perspective. It should bring freedom to experiment for God's glory, to risk and possibly fail, all in anticipation of what the Spirit might do in our midst. (Watters 2007, 1–2)

About the same time, Watters was drawn to the extraordinary imagery in Revelation 5:1–10, where the Lion of the tribe of Judah, the Lion of one ethnic group, appears also as the Lamb who "purchased for God members of every tribe and language and people and nation" (v. 9). The Lamb was the Lamb of all ethnic groups, all localities. Moved by the description in Revelation 7:9 of a multitude before the throne of God and before the Lamb, in quantity beyond count, and in quality from "every nation, tribe, people and language," Watters saw in this imagery an extraordinary vision of what God intends to achieve among humankind.

Also during this time, a colleague gave Watters a copy of *Built to Last*, by Jim Collins and Jerry I. Porras (1994), and asked him to read it in preparation for some planning meetings. Having more urgent things to do, he set it aside until he was packing for his flight from Nairobi to Los Angeles to attend these meetings. Putting the book into his bag, he thought that he would at least skim it before he arrived. However, on the plane he began to read it, and God spoke to him through this business book in a special way over the next twenty-four hours before he arrived in Los Angeles. What he read challenged him to reflect on Wycliffe's core purpose and values and to consider audacious goals. Watters realized that his organization was no longer experiencing an acceleration in the pace of Bible translation. He also recognized that at its current pace it would take 100 to 150 years before every language community needing translation would even begin a translation program. Without dreams of what God might do through Wycliffe, there was little likelihood of change.

Watters pondered the contrast between secular organizations that could have audacious visions and an organization such as Wycliffe, dedicated to the Lord of the universe but seemingly satisfied with only incremental change. In considering what an audacious goal for Wycliffe might be, he formed a question on that flight from Nairobi to Los Angeles: "What would we have to do so that by the year 2025 every language needing Scripture has a Bible or a New Testament or relevant portions or at least a translation program in progress? This would shorten the waiting process by one hundred years or more if the vision embedded inside this question was realized" (Watters 2007, 3).

As Watters listened to the Holy Spirit and began to sketch out this vision, he was also challenged by doubt. He expected that most people in the organization would not embrace it. He knew that if this was to become a corporate vision, it had to be embraced by many others. It would not be a vision if it came only from his voice. The voice of others would be the Spirit's confirmation, one way or the other.

> I could imagine most of the arguments against it. How can this be feasible? Would the quality of translations be jeopardized? Would we have to give up some of our historic structures and policies? And so on. I expected resistance to what was implied in the question to be significant. The biggest change required us to recognize we could not accomplish this vision on our own. We needed to depend on God and

to partner with others in new ways. But most radically, we would have to include people from the worldwide church in ways we never had done before. The majority of Christians were now in Africa, Asia, and Latin America, not North America and Europe. We would have to open our doors in new ways to Africans, Asians, Latin Americans, and Pacific Islanders. We had to ask ourselves: Who has God called to be part of his workforce to accomplish the translation of his word around the world? (Watters 2007, 4)

As Watters prayed about this, he felt compelled by the Spirit to present this new vision, yet he was uncertain. Probably few people, if any, would embrace it.

Watters describes how, with much trepidation, he presented a draft of this vision for a radical change in focus to a few key leaders. To his astonishment, they all responded positively. Some said immediately that they wanted to be part of it. Others said they too had been troubled in spirit by the slowing pace of Bible translation. Others had been seeking direction from the Holy Spirit for change. With this encouragement, Watters began preparation for the 1999 corporate conference, where representatives from around the world would vote to accept or reject a vision to dramatically expand the translation workforce. He prepared drafts of the vision statement and shared it with members of the board and international leaders, inviting their feedback. He asked them to pray with him that God would move his people to a new vision of their work. In the end well over one hundred people contributed to the final document with their questions and comments. During the conference, a special prayer team prayed for wisdom, as did the conference delegates and many not present.

When the moment came for a conference committee to present a carefully crafted resolution of what had become known as Vision 2025 (sidebar 2.1), the Holy Spirit once again moved in power. Although the discussion was at times intense, when the time came for the vote, the conference was nearly unanimous in its affirmation of the new vision. In his twenty-two years of attending international corporate conferences, Watters had never seen such a thing take place. He had expected to spend much of his eight-year tenure revising the vision until it was acceptable and approved. Instead he began his eight-year tenure as executive director with clear affirmation by the conference

---

Sidebar 2.1   Vision 2025: Wycliffe's Conference Resolution

Watters 2007, 5

Motivated by the pressing need for all peoples to have access to the Word of God in a language that speaks to their hearts, and reaffirming our historic values and our trust in God to accomplish the impossible,

We embrace the vision that by the year 2025 a Bible translation project will be in progress for every people group that needs it.

We acknowledge that this cannot be accomplished simply by our working harder or doing more of what we are now doing. It will require us to make significant changes in our attitudes and ways of working.

Our desire is to build capacity for sustainable Bible translation programs and Scripture-use activities. Therefore, we urge each entity within our family of organizations to give priority to strengthening present partnerships, forming additional strategic partnerships, and working together to develop creative approaches appropriate to each context.

To this end we commit ourselves to pray for the fulfillment of this vision, seeking God's guidance and obeying Him in whatever new directions He may lead.

---

of a vision that called for profound changes in direction in the years to come. Watters shares the following perspectives on this vision.

We recognized that the Vision would be achieved only if God desired to see it achieved. It would only be possible if more than Wycliffe was involved. And it would only be possible if we learned to work differently. In terms of resources to achieve the Vision, all the Bible translation agencies around the world did not have sufficient resources. But God did. He had more than sufficient resources in his worldwide church. It would depend on the church's vision to see all people have access to the Word of God in their own language. Working differently would require partnering more closely with various organizations that had similar concerns for the peoples of the earth without adequate access to the Word of God. Ultimately, Vision 2025 called for a posture or attitude before God that said we were available for him to use, and we were ready to change in whatever ways he desired. At that time we spoke of over 4,000 languages without a Bible or New Testament, representing around a billion people. We also said that over 2,000 of those languages still did not have any translation program in progress.

Later we increased the number to 3,000 languages with no program in progress, representing some 300 million people. (Watters 2007, 6)

Vision and corporate prayer are inextricably linked. God clarifies vision within and through corporate prayer. God motivates people to action through corporate prayer. Prayer is the body of Christ humbling itself before God, worshiping God, listening to the Holy Spirit, and submitting in obedience to the will and purpose of God. John Watters found that prayer became the driving energy for the vision God had given him. In fact, three years after the adoption of Vision 2025, he challenged participants at the next Wycliffe International conference to renew their awareness of their dependence on God by stating, "Prayer is our greatest strategic response and our greatest resource, because it brings us right into the presence of God himself. In prayer we acknowledge our total dependence on him and our desire to see him glorified above all else" (Watters 2007, 7). The representatives responded by passing only one resolution at that conference, committing themselves and calling their leaders to model and prioritize prayer in all aspects of work and ministry.

Watters reports that every advance toward Vision 2025 followed significant times of working together in prayer, substantive listening to one another, and then moving forward in multiple dramas that were often painful and challenging. Partnership development, essential to the new paradigm, pushed workers to rethink their relationships with outsiders and to relinquish some of the standard ways of doing things. Learning to trust through relationships and prayer, they opened their hands and hearts to new people and new ways of working.

My Vision or God's Vision?

When I accepted the position of dean of the School of World Mission at Fuller in 1999, many people asked me, "What is your vision for the school?" I struggled to answer that question, and I usually responded by saying that I didn't know enough about the faculty, the students, and the changing face of missions to give a good answer, but in a year or so I would be ready to respond. Today I would answer differently. I believe that the only vision of value for Christian ministry is God's vision, and that vision is given not to individuals but rather to the body of Christ. God uses individuals, such as Gupta and Watters, to be a catalyst within the "body," but God's vision is always to his church and for his church. In my former role as dean, my work should have been listening to the Holy Spirit and God's people and serving as a catalyst to help the community discern together the role and work we must share under the reign of God.

At the time I was doing the final editing on this book, a visiting Asian leader who had been teaching in a school started by one of his peers said to me, "I left that school because the leader's vision was different from mine." When a leader speaks of "my vision," the leader sets up a dichotomy between those who agree and follow and those who do not. The natural outcome of "my vision" is that it is different from "her vision," and these differences create division and conflict. My perspective here is that the only vision worth following is God's vision, and God reveals that vision to many, not just one.

Kingdom work requires the body of Christ to respond to God's call and commit to corporate action—a community of prayer, faith, and trust engaged in the mission of God. Without vision, the community loses its sense of purpose and direction. Without prayer, the community loses its humility, essential for trust, and its faith to step out together in action. God calls apostolic leaders, in the power of the Holy Spirit, to renew the vision of the body of Christ, and to invite God's people to engage together in prayer and obedience to work together as a missional community. However, neither Bobby Gupta nor John Watters could claim the vision as his own. Each was led by the Holy Spirit to seek the counsel and wisdom of others. Each found the vision changing and growing as he engaged others in the community of believers. God used each man as a catalyst within his community to challenge the status quo, and then to call people together to listen as God spoke to them through the Spirit. The people who shaped the visions that emerged in India and in Wycliffe International then committed themselves to years of setting foundations, calling thousands to come together to seek God's direction in prayer, and then mobilizing and equipping God's people to engage together for the mission of God. In Wycliffe the work of Bible translation gained a momentum most had thought impossible a decade earlier, and in India over a period of twenty-five years men and women of God across the country planted more than two hundred thousand churches.

3

Kingdom Values and Rewards

Conflict about Priorities: A Case Study

"How can Segu let his brother take the motorcycle off to his village for the weekend?" Je Syun said angrily to partner Jang Chul.

"Doesn't he know it's for evangelistic trips and not for personal use?" Jang Chul couldn't offer any consolation. Little irksome frustrations had been accumulating over the months, and both he and Je Syun were frazzled.

Je Syun and Jang Chul had come to Africa with their wives and children with a vision to serve God through evangelism and development work. Leaving homes, family, and good jobs in Korea, they had accepted an assignment to work in a hot, dry North African nation to show mercy and share the gospel. During their language-learning period, they met Segu, a Muslim convert who had become a national missionary, supported by a national mission board. Segu sensed God had gifted him in evangelism, and he was happy to partner with his new Korean friends. They worked together for over three years and enjoyed each other's friendship. They were thankful to God for their partnership and the challenging task they shared.

As members of the HOSANNAH mission, Je Syun and Jang Chul were supported through donations from friends and churches in Korea. They received donations for both personal and project expenses, and

Je Syun and Jang Chul lived comfortably with their families in spite of local poverty, bad roads, and sporadic electricity. They even had enough money to fund evangelism trips with nationals, such as Segu, and a few development projects, such as the wells that were being dug in one of the villages. The one luxury they enjoyed was importing some special Korean food that helped them endure the challenges of this difficult place.

Segu, in contrast, lived on a limited salary from his mission. He and his family had built a mud-brick house, and in his yard they had dug a pit toilet and a well that gave murky water for washing and cooking. He had no electricity. As he went about his evangelistic ministries, he spent much time and energy using public transportation to reach the various villages that had been targeted for evangelism and development survey work. After long trips, Segu returned home exhausted and often fell ill. Segu couldn't help wondering why his Korean friends had so much and he had so little. He complained to God and asked God to provide more support for his ministry.

After a while Je Syun observed that the time Segu spent traveling had a negative effect on the team's goals, and he felt that the team could not afford to waste time. Je Syun offered to try to obtain funding for a motorcycle for the projects. Segu was very pleased with this. Within a few months, word came that a donor had agreed to fund a motorcycle for both the evangelism trips and one of the clean-water projects. Je Syun entrusted the motorcycle to Segu because he and Jang Chul each had their own personal vehicle that their donors had provided.

After a few months, Je Syun and Jang Chul noticed that frequently Segu's brother used the motorcycle for personal business. This occurred over an extended period of time, and Je Syun's frustration mounted as he noticed the pattern. Finally, he decided he had to address the issue head on. He asked Segu, "Why do you let your brother use your motorcycle all the time? Don't you know it was given to the project to be used for project needs?" Segu answered, "But . . . he's my brother."

Cultural Values and Kingdom Work

What are the cultural values that we bring to kingdom work? Some of the questions that arise from the case study are the following:

1. Je Syun and Jang Chul left home, family, and work for the gospel—what kind of support is appropriate for this sacrifice?
2. Segu asked, "They have much; why don't I get more to help me and my family?"
3. The missionaries and Segu disagreed about the question, how should ministry resources be shared between workers and family?

The typical values that relate to work concern our priorities for schedules, the kinds of processes we use to get work done, relationships that we have for working together, the routines that make up work in any given situation, and how we use and share the resources we have for ministry. People working in multicultural teams often have substantive disagreements about core values on these priorities.

In 2000, my wife, Judy, and I conducted a workshop in Cameroon that brought together Western and African partners from fourteen different African countries. The Western participants in this conference were members of a nongovernmental organization (NGO) working to provide Scriptures and literacy for African churches, and the African partners were part of national organizations of churches in each of these countries that were working in parallel and support relationships with NGOs. At the beginning of the workshop, I separated the Western participants and the African participants and gave them the assignment to define what partnership means. I asked for three specific responses: (1) define a partnership, (2) describe the character qualities that you would like your partners to have, and (3) explain what you would expect to give others in a partnership relationship. The responses to these questions are summarized in table 3.1.

Table 3.1 Contrasting Partnership Assumptions

Western Partners	African Partners
• Definition—task, results	• Definition—relational ministry
• Character—reliability, humility, commitment, <u>work values</u>	• Character—love, call of God, generosity, <u>social values</u>
• Give—<u>superior/inferior,</u> training, money, facilitation, <u>critical feedback</u>	• Give—<u>complementary,</u> people, relationships, spiritual resources, <u>everything is shared</u>

The definition of "partnership" varied significantly between the Western and the African partners. The Westerners defined partnership as relationships to complete the task, enabling the NGO to achieve its outcomes in as timely a way as possible. The African partners defined partnership as relations of commitment to God and to one another for the work of ministry. The Western partners agreed that partnership was not like marriage, whereas African partners asserted that it was like marriage.

The character qualities sought by these partners in the "other partners" also differed. The Western partners emphasized character qualities that focused on work values—reliability, enough humility to accept advice and direction, and commitment to the achievement of partnership goals. The African partners emphasized social values. They wanted to work with people who manifested the calling of God, showed love for one another, and were generous.

In response to the question, what would you give your partners? the Western partners defined "giving" in terms that emphasized their superior position in the relationship. The Western partners offered training, money, and facilitation of the project. They also proposed critical feedback to assure that the project achieved the quality of goals to which they aspired. These are exactly the kinds of gifts that Je Syun and Jang Chul gave to Segu in the opening case study—support for a motorcycle and ministry projects and critical feedback about how Segu used these resources.

The African partners emphasized relationships that were complementary, meaning mutual sharing of differences in kind, but of equal value and priority. Each partner contributes people with differing gifts, relationships essential to community and work, and the spiritual resources of a Christian community. The African partners valued open sharing of all available resources in a process that emphasizes mutual, rather than superior/inferior, relationship. Segu's concern in the story focused on the lack of mutual sharing and the exclusion of family from one's network of sharing.

One might suggest that the Africans emphasized more spiritual things than the Westerners, and in one sense that was true. However, both African and Western partners defined giving in terms of their particular cultural bias and worldview. The culture of the

African partners values reciprocity in relationships, and they find social relationships more important than task-oriented activities. Therefore, they commit time and priority to relational goals and relational objectives. The Western partners have a culture that focuses on performance, getting things done, and doing work with emphasis on quality, commitment, and productivity. We can see, then, the significant contrast between these two groups regarding the values of work.

What Is Kingdom Partnership?

Which of these partners is more committed to kingdom partnership? After working with both groups intensely over a period of two weeks, I concluded that neither of them had a clear understanding of what kingdom partnerships involve. In our discussions about working relationships, they all clung to their cultural values and their understandings of how to go about work. They did not budge in their self-assurance that their way of doing things was the best for the goals that they sought to achieve together. They dialogued civilly, debated with one another about goals, and even appeared to make some compromises. However, when they returned to their work situations, they defaulted to their prior attitudes and practices and continued to do things as they had done them earlier.

At the beginning of a two-week workshop, they acknowledged their failure to work effectively together, and after the workshop, they continued the work patterns they had brought with them when they came. They were unable to negotiate effectively either their cultural differences or their spiritual commitments in order to engage together in kingdom work.

Table 3.2 suggests some of the contrasts between what constitutes work driven by cultural values and that driven by kingdom values. Both the African and the Western partners in this African context gave greater priority to their cultural values for working relationships than to kingdom values. The partners were concerned about their national identities and gave those identities priority over their Christian identity. They persisted in clinging to the way they had done things before they began the partnership. It was more important to be American or Swiss or Ivorian or Ghanaian than it was to focus on their common identity as Christians.

Table 3.2 Cultural and Kingdom Values in Partner Relations

Cultural Values	Kingdom Values
• Defend identity (nationalism)	• Deny self (member of body)
• Control process	• Release control
• Critique other	• Serve others
• Achieve ends	• Trust God for ends

The Westerners who represented the mission organization persisted in their need to control the process of the partnership. They refused to bend on the structures and processes that were part of how they worked and insisted on and defended these processes as essential to assuring the quality of their work. Both sets of partners critiqued the other and the flaws and difficulties in their working relationships. The Africans saw the Westerners as harsh, unbending, and uncaring; the Westerners saw the Africans as undisciplined, careless about time, and having low goals with regard to productivity.

Each of these partners was more focused on achieving the ends that each had for partnership than on developing effective relationships together. Like the Korean Je Syun in the case study, the Western partners were concerned about task and project goals, whereas the African partners were concerned about their working relationships, their financial needs, and the relational benefits of being engaged in a partnership. Each was unwilling to change these priorities, and they readily judged and condemned the partners regarding these disagreements.

Jesus on Kingdom Values

Jesus is quite clear about the values he expects of those who want to follow him in the work of the kingdom. The most important statement is the one that he makes to his disciples when they begin to understand that he is the Christ. "Those who would be my disciples must deny themselves and take up their cross daily and follow me.

For those who want to save their life will lose it, but those who lose their life for me will save it" (Luke 9:23–24). This denying of self is the foundation for other key values and actions that follow.

A core kingdom value is serving others. Jesus makes this very clear to his disciples when they are fighting with one another about who is going to be the greatest in the kingdom of heaven. Darrell Guder notes that Jesus absolutely rejects the social practices of domination and ruling over others that characterize culture, practices we often carry into our relationships with partners in the work of the kingdom (2000, 138). "Instead, whoever wants to become great among you must be your servant, and whoever wants to be first must be your slave—just as the Son of Man did not come to be served, but to serve, and to give his life as a ransom for many" (Matt. 20:26–28). This character of serving others does not mean Western missionaries cannot critique African work, or that Africans should not disagree with a missionary's approach to doing a job. Rather, the issue is whether we act from positions of domination and resistance or from positions of service.

Another core kingdom value is relinquishing control of the process, encapsulated in Jesus's statement, "whoever loses their life for me will save it" (Luke 9:24). In our efforts to save our lives, we become focused on controlling what happens around us. The Koreans and Westerners in our case studies strove to achieve outcomes that fulfilled their personal sense of calling, ownership, and security. When we focus on letting go, living and working at risk, then we no longer need to control. Kingdom work demands that we shift our focus from securing to losing our lives in pursuit of the mission of God.

Finally, we must submit our value for achievement to the kingdom priority of trusting God for all outcomes. Since it is God's kingdom and God's Spirit who is moving us, God is responsible for the results. Je Syun was anxious about "project needs," and the Western partners were anxious about the quality of African technical work. Segu complained about having little, and African partners felt diminished in their partnership roles. As servants we need not be anxious or diminished when we are engaged in kingdom work. God is wholly capable of accomplishing all that he intends, and God values the work of all partners equally. Our task is to trust God and believe that he will accomplish his purpose in the service that we do.

I have often thought that Phillip Yancey's notion of the logic of "ungrace" is a very appropriate description of the way cultures work (Yancey 1997, 83–90). People use their cultural values and systems to critique those who fail to live up to their rules, to judge and condemn based upon appearances, and to punish failure to conform by inflicting emotional and physical pain. Kingdom values, in contrast, employ the illogic of grace. When we follow God's way, we focus on loving one another and extending grace to our brothers and sisters in contexts where we have disagreements and conflicts with them. We try to implement the commands of the Lord to love one another, to deny ourselves, and to be servants. Our relationships are then guided not by logic but by the illogic of love that flows from grace.

What Will We Get for Kingdom Work?

For the kingdom of heaven is like a landowner who went out early in the morning to hire workers for his vineyard. He had agreed to pay them a denarius for the day and sent them into his vineyard.

About nine in the morning he went out and saw others standing in the marketplace doing nothing. He told them, "You also go and work in my vineyard, and I will pay you whatever is right." And so they went.

He went out again about noon and about three in the afternoon and did the same thing. About five in the afternoon he went out and found still others standing around. He asked them, "Why have you been standing here all day long doing nothing?"

"Because no one hired us," they answered.

He said to them, "You also go and work in my vineyard."

When evening came, the owner of the vineyard said to his supervisor, "Call the workers and pay them their wages, beginning with the last ones hired and going on to the first."

The workers who were hired about five in the afternoon came and each one received a denarius. So when those came who were hired first, they expected to receive more. But each one of them also received a denarius. When they received it, they began to grumble against the landowner. "These men who were hired last worked only one hour," they said, "and you have made them equal to us who have borne the burden of the work and the heat of the day."

But he answered one of them, "Friend, I am not being unfair to you. Didn't you agree to work for a denarius? Take your pay and go. I want to give the man who was hired last the same as I gave you. Don't I have the right to do what I want with my own money? Or are you envious because I am generous?"

So the last shall be first, and the first will be last. (Matt. 20:1–16)

When Jesus tells the story of the landowner hiring men to work in his vineyard, he is answering a question that Peter raised earlier in Matthew 19:27. Jesus and the disciples had just encountered the rich young man who asked Jesus what he should do to inherit eternal life. When Jesus told the man to sell everything he had and give his money to the poor, the man walked away sadly. Peter then turned to Jesus and asked, "We have left everything to follow you! What then will there be for us?" Most people who engage in ministry occasionally ask this question. In fact, as we follow the story, Jesus addresses a series of what I call "human questions" about work and reward. These questions parallel those Je Syun, Jang Chul, and Segu asked in the opening case study of the chapter:

1. What will I (we) get for our labor? (Matt. 19:27)
2. Why don't I get more? (Matt. 20:11)
3. What is fair? (Matt. 20:12)
4. In view of our willingness to sacrifice all, will you give us more than the rest? (Matt. 20:21–22)

When we organize partnerships for cross-cultural ministry, people in those partnerships always want to know what they are going to get for their participation. This often becomes a source of negotiation and conflict. In that conflict, people generally ask the question, why don't I get more? Because we have different cultural values about labor and compensation, these questions become even more pressing than they are within the same cultural context.

As we look at Westerners and Asians working in Africa or in developing countries such as Papua New Guinea, Indonesia, and

Cambodia, the difference in financial support for expatriate missionaries and local people is significant. Local people often ask, what is fair? Just as in the case of Segu, they don't understand why Westerners or Koreans should be paid so much for their work while they are paid so little.

Finally, many who make significant sacrifices fall into the same trap that James and John did when they asked Jesus, "Will you give us more than the rest (seats at your right and left hand)?" What "more than the rest" means may vary from group to group, organization to organization. In my experience, many Christians feel that working harder and sacrificing more somehow obligates God to give them a better standing with Christ and a bigger welcome when they enter into the kingdom. They feel that the quality of their performance certainly warrants more than their "poor performing" brothers and sisters will receive.

Jesus answers all these questions in the text, so let's see how he responds to them. First is the question, "We have left everything. What will there be for us?" Jesus responds (Matt. 19:28–30) that while they have left everything, they have left nothing. Assuring them that they cannot out-give God, he promises that they will sit with him in his glorious throne in heaven. Further, he proclaims that everything they have given up—houses, brothers and sisters, father and mother, or children—will be returned to them a hundred times more, and they will "inherit eternal life." The essence of Jesus's declaration is that our "sacrifices" are not sacrifices at all. Rather, when we are willing to obey God and relinquish those things that possess us, God replaces them with much more. Yet, he confounds them and us when he concludes, "But many who are first will be last, and many who are last will be first" (Matt. 19:30).

In the story of the day laborers, they ask, why don't I get more? Those who started early in the morning are angry that they received the same pay as those who worked only an hour at the end of the day. In cross-cultural ministries people who come from the workaholic cultures of the West often express frustration with non-Western co-laborers who don't work as long or as hard as they do. Critical of their non-Western neighbors, they see their own work habits as better than those of the local people and feel that they have a right to more. In our readiness to judge, we forget that the measure that we use will be turned against us. When we assume that our brothers are unspiritual because they do not share our "work ethic," we are judging and condemning them on the basis of our own standards. Jesus states clearly that we should not judge (Matt. 7:1–3).

These same laborers then complain about fairness. They say to the landowner, "You have made them equal to us who have borne the burden of the work and the heat of the day" (Matt. 20:12). The owner replies, "I am not being unfair to you. . . . Don't I have the right to do what I want with my own money? Or are you envious because I am generous? So the last will be first, and the first will be last" (Matt. 20:13–16). The landowner in Jesus's story represents God reigning in the kingdom of God. The landowner agrees with those who came first that they should work for a day's wage, and in his generosity he pays them all a day's wage. The point of this story is that God is generous to all, regardless of our performance.

Some have interpreted this text to refer primarily to God's gift of salvation to those who make decisions at the end of their lives. While this application is certainly true, the context of the story is clearly part of Jesus's answer to Peter's question, "We have left everything to follow you! What then will there be for us?" (Matt. 19:27). Jesus is speaking about present and future rewards for those who join him in proclaiming the "good news of the kingdom."

Kingdom Rewards?

Peter's question, "What will we get?" is answered definitively in Jesus's response to James and John on their request for seats at his right and left hand in the kingdom. Jesus says to them, "Can you drink the cup I am going to drink?" (Matt. 20:22). When they say, "We can," he assures them that they will drink that cup, but that he cannot grant their request. Rather, he challenges their basic values. "Whoever wants to become great among you must be your servant, and whoever wants to be first must be your slave—just as the Son of Man did not come to be served, but to serve, and to give his life as a ransom for many" (Matt. 20:26–28).

In summary, Jesus makes the following points about kingdom work:

1. He calls many diverse people to work. (Matt. 20:3–6)
2. He pays "whatever is right." (Matt. 20:4)
3. He is generous but not "fair." (Matt. 20:13–15)
4. He gives "a hundred times as much." (Matt. 19:29)
5. He gives "his life as a ransom for many." (Matt. 20:28)

We can see that the values Jesus proclaims contradict most cultural values about how we work. Unless we understand the priorities that God has for our working relationships, we will always distort them and instead use our values about rewards and expectations to guide us as we seek to negotiate our work together.

As we reflect on the case study of Segu, Je Syun, and Jang Chul, what would be different if they oriented their relationships around these kingdom priorities? The first step they must all take is to focus on their relationship with God and then with one another. This is the only way they can achieve mutual understanding and acceptance of their worldview differences. With God as the central person in their relationships, it will be possible to become more generous toward one another. This generosity for Segu would mean thanksgiving for the blessings his Korean brothers have received; for Je Syun and Jang Chul, it would mean sharing more of their abundance with their brother Segu. Out of understanding and generosity, they would all discover more mutual trust: trust that accepts difference in patterns of work, trust that forgives the weaknesses of the other, and trust that focuses on God to accomplish their common mission. And Je Syun could ask Segu, "How can we help you to support and encourage your brother? We want him to know that we love him as you do." If they together made these commitments, their ministries would flourish as the people of God, motivated together, achieved the purpose of God in their projects and teamwork.

Part 2

Building Trust

4

The Necessity of Learning

Aukan Translation Project: A Case Study

Louis had proposed a partnership with leaders of the Aukan church over several months, but the pastors just didn't seem to be interested. He discussed with them the value of having Scripture in their language, and they agreed. He explained about the time and cost of a translation project and the importance of their involvement. He asked them about the two young men he had chosen to work with him, and on this they clearly voiced their opposition. When he explained that these young men could read and write in the Dutch and Aukan languages, and that they had college-level training, key qualifications to serve as mother-tongue translators, the pastors were not impressed. They said these men had yet to prove themselves responsible and faithful to the Lord and the church.

When I arrived in Suriname to conduct a workshop, Louis explained the situation to me and asked if I had any ideas about how he might encourage these leaders to get behind the project and provide partial support for these two young men, who had already begun training for translation. We agreed to invite Pastor Waksam to lunch and talk to him about the program.

On the appointed day, we met Pastor Waksam at a local restaurant in the city. Over lunch Louis introduced me, and we began to share with each other a few of the details of our lives. I learned that Pastor Waksam had served many years in the mother church in the city before the elders asked him to lead the second Aukan church. Throughout that time, he had a job with the government that provided support for his family. He explained that the normal lunch hour was from noon to 3:00 p.m., and that he used this time to visit the sick and care for people in his congregation. As we talked, I asked him if he was paid for his church ministry. He replied, "Not one cent." When we asked why, he quoted Colossians 3:23, saying that all the men and women who worked for the church were "working for the Lord."

When I had visited the church a few days earlier, I had observed an organizational chart showing all the ministries of this local congregation, so I asked him how he chose the people to lead these ministries. He explained that he and the other elders made these decisions together. Each person chosen to lead a ministry had demonstrated faithful service to the Lord, serving in a variety of ways over a long period of time. When he and the elders were confident of their faithfulness and commitment, people were then invited to take a ministry leadership role. At that point I asked how long they might observe a person before they invited him or her to lead. Pastor Waksam replied, "About ten years."

As Louis and I drove back to the translation center, Louis said to me, "Not one cent! No wonder they rejected my request to provide 10 percent of the salary of my translators. And ten years! No wonder these guys have not proven themselves faithful and qualified for leadership. They are only twenty and twenty-one years old."

Social Games of Leadership

Leading cross-culturally is inspiring people who come from two or more cultural traditions to *participate with you in building a community of trust* and then to follow you and be empowered by you to achieve a compelling vision of faith. The problem Louis faced as leader of the Aukan translation project was his lack of understanding about Aukan expectations for leadership, and from that his failure to inspire trust and support for the translation project. Working from assumptions that he shared with other members of his organization, he organized the project according to the technical requirements of the task and recruited the men he felt best qualified to do the job. Although he expected to raise funds to pay these men, he had hoped that the strong Aukan churches in the capital city would support it financially as well. He assumed that if they engaged financially, they would have a stronger commitment to the final published New Testament. Our brief "learning lunch" shattered all his assumptions about that cooperation. The only point of agreement was that Louis should indeed supervise the project and that his organization should pay these laborers for their work.

The case study illustrates how our cultural assumptions are incredibly useful in one context and incredibly misleading in another. Louis's culture, an American in Wycliffe Bible Translators, defined for him a legitimate social structure and process for relationships and work; within that structure the players know what to value and which incentives motivate others for the common good. Yet, when the context changed to Aukan society and churches, none of Louis's assumptions could be applied with validity in the new situation.

Culture is both our palace and our prison (Lingenfelter 1998, 20). As a "palace," it supplies all the essential needs for life—structure, order, access to materials, and predictability in our relationships, and comfort, meaning, accountability, and significance in our personal lives. However, humans, with their marvelous God-given creativity, have elaborated this need and capacity for culture to design wonderfully varied and even unique sociocultural systems. Thus our unique "personal culture" and shared "ethnic or national culture," used as our guiding compass for life, work, and relationships, fails utterly when taken beyond the context in which it was created and refined. Culture becomes a "prison" to us when we insist on employing its structure, order, meanings, and values to all of our life experiences. Although that tendency is not so damaging to those who live their entire lives in one locality, for those who venture into the world of mission, and who seek to partner with others in the global body of Christ, such behavior leads to disaster in relationships and the practice of ministry.

Early in my career, I often described culture as simply a neutral set of concepts and propositions that we use to organize our lives, interpret our experience, and evaluate the behavior of others. The first problem with this definition is that it limits our understanding of culture to the mind—"concepts and propositions." From the vantage point of 2008, I prefer to speak of sociocultural systems in which human ideas and social interests intersect in the bodies of persons and social community. In this book we will examine how people achieve social interests through "social games" that structure social life and values, and how they organize, interpret, and evaluate these experiences through a "worldview" comprised of concepts, beliefs, and propositions expressed in their language and communication.

The second problem with my early definition is the idea that culture is "neutral." After years of reflection on texts of Scripture that reference the world, ideas, doctrines, ancestors, myths, and genealogies, I have concluded that Scripture takes a rather negative stance toward the fallen human cultural ways of life. More specifically, Peter writes that we have been "redeemed from the empty way of life handed down to you from your ancestors" (1 Pet. 1:18). We must understand that Peter is not suggesting that we abandon cultural life, which indeed is God's gift to humanity, but rather that we must recognize the difference between the "empty way of life" that results from rebellion against God and the redeemed life of obedience in Christ. In a similar vein, Paul notes that "God has bound everyone over to disobedience so that he may have mercy on them all" (Rom. 11:32) and then challenges us: "Do not conform to the pattern of this world, but be transformed by the renewing of your mind" (Rom. 12:2).

As Louis and I debriefed our lunch conversation with Pastor Waksam, I gently explained to Louis that he should not be surprised at his misunderstanding. Blinded by his own cultural assumptions and practices, he could not have known, without asking, what Waksam and the Aukan people expected of him or the translation project. Further, learning how Aukans think about and exercise leadership takes more intentional observation and inquiry. Our first step in this process over lunch demonstrated why learning is essential to effective cross-cultural leadership.

Social Games and Culture

When the team or ministry community is comprised of people from two or more cultures, a would-be leader must spend time learning about the "social game" assumptions of these diverse people. We have observed in the Aukan translation case that Louis failed to gain Aukan support for his translation project, in large part because he did not understand how to seek support within the Aukan social game of church and leadership. Understanding social games is both a simple and a challenging exercise.

I will use the analogy of sports to illustrate this point. Mary Douglas (1982) notes that all human societies must make fundamental choices about the degree to which relationships are defined by role and rule (Grid), and the degree to which group interests have priority over individual interests (Group). Together these two variables limit social life to four, and only four, primary structures for social engagement. I have called these alternatives "prototype social games" to signal that people may learn and play more than one, and that these social arrangements may occur side by side in social community. Douglas also notes that each of these primary structures generates a distinctive *cultural bias* comprised of specific values and a specific worldview resulting from social choices.

Using examples from sports games, figure 4.1 defines some of the essential features of each of these social arrangements. American baseball emphasizes specialized roles for each player and individual performance. In baseball the manager directs the flow of the game, intervening to change pitchers, substitute hitters, and manage team play. In contrast, in American football or international soccer, team play is essential in every aspect of the game, and leadership resides with the players on the field. In American football, the quarterback and the defensive captain call for offensive and defensive formations, in consultation with the team coaches, but have the freedom to make situational decisions.

Volleyball is clearly a game of team play. Although Olympic volleyball defines specialized roles for players, the "camp" volleyball game requires every player to play every position and rotate throughout the game. This social arrangement Douglas calls "egalitarian." Golf is obviously an individual game in which each individual plays against himself or herself using past performance as the measure of success or failure, and in match play, performing at a level superior to the other individuals playing. The social structures of these games illustrate the "prototypes" employed by people around the world as they frame the complexities of social life.

Figure 4.1 The Prototype Social Games

Bureaucratic Game	+	Corporate Game
Baseball	G R I D	*Football and Soccer*
• Specialized roles		• Specialized roles
• Best performance wins		• Best team play wins
• Manager directs game		• Best players lead
– GROUP		GROUP +
Individualist Game	G R I D	Collectivist Game
Golf		*Volleyball*
• Each individual in		• Everybody plays every
match play		position and rotates

Learning the Social Games of Culture

I first observed the game of cricket when I spent the summer of 1978 in England. Just from watching on the edge of the field, I learned that two teams, dressed in white, played a ball game in which a "bowler" from one team threw the ball toward a "wicket" of stakes placed in the ground, defended by a batsman from the other team. If the batsman hit the ball, he would run to the opposite wicket while the players in the field chased the ball and attempted to catch it and to knock down the wicket before the batter could get back to defend it. Watching from the sidelines, without anyone to help me understand the game, I could only interpret it from my knowledge of American baseball. This proved to be a very confusing exercise. Although some aspects of the game were similar—throwing and hitting a ball, fielding hit balls, and catching a hit ball before it touched the ground, thereby causing the batter to sit down—nothing else made sense to me. To understand the game, I had to find a knowledgeable person to explain the rules of the game and the strategies that players use to win. I never did take the time to learn more, and although I have watched a couple of movies that feature cricket, I still do not understand the game.

Most missionaries learn the social games of nationals the way I learned about cricket. They watch church or leadership events as spectators, they may have a casual conversation with someone about what is happening, they may even learn to know who are the best players, but they rarely take time to learn the rules of the game and the strategies players use to win.

To gain a deeper understanding, it is necessary to watch more carefully, make notes on what you observe, and then ask questions. When Louis and I went to lunch with Pastor Waksam, we had already observed a group of men working at the church, and we had seen the organizational chart and learned about some of the ministries of the church just by visiting the pastor's office. The lunch presented the opportunity to ask four basic questions:

1. How did you become a leader?
2. What are the qualities you look for in leaders?
3. How do you and your congregation select others to lead ministries?
4. How are they compensated or rewarded for serving?

As Pastor Waksam answered these questions, we learned some very important facts about the social game of the Aukan church (see figure 4.2).

Figure 4.2 Wycliffe/Aukan Games of Work

Bureaucratic Game *Project Management* • Task, skill authority • Delegated power • Decision from supervisor • Structural support	GRID +	Corporate Game
− GROUP		GROUP +
Individualist Game	GRID −	Collectivist Game *Aukan Management* • Personal authority • Allocated power • Consensus decisions • Symbolic support

Pastor Waksam's life and ministry demonstrated what he had told us about all Aukan leaders—authority is personal; every person earns the right to lead by serving others in the church over many years. His comment about watching a person for ten years specified the length of time and the level of trust required to become a pastor or leader in ministry. Second, we learned that the group allocates power to these leaders by consensus. They observe together, evaluate together, and agree together about who is serving well and who should be entrusted with more. Finally, we learned that the rewards of leadership are symbolic—they are all "working for the Lord," and that is reward enough. For the sake of comparison, I call this a "collectivist" social game.

Louis, in contrast, brought "bureaucratic game" assumptions to the translation task (figure 4.2). He, in consultation with his supervisor (delegated authority), chose to hire two young Aukan Christians because of their education and language skills. He intended to train them in the essential linguistic skills to serve as mother-tongue translators. Louis made decisions about the project using the hierarchical structure and resources of the organization of which he was a part.

Learning That Builds Trust

One of the distortions that we as human beings bring to social relationships is that of making our familiar structure the only structure that God can use to accomplish his purpose. We distort the diversity of God's creation and reduce the structures for human life to those that are familiar to us. By denying the validity of other structures, we force people to submit to our standards and structures of relationship in order to accomplish the work and purpose of God.

The case of the Aukan translation project shows how learning and accepting the Aukan structure of church and leadership were especially important to gain the trust and support of Aukan leaders. Louis and his Wycliffe colleagues had to engage in relationships with several different ethnic churches, each with its unique version of one of the four prototype social games. As a translation organization, they had their own vision, goals, structure, and processes, which were different from those of all the churches with which they sought to partner. As they committed to work together, they often struggled with disagreements about goals, structures, and processes, each side seeing its own as the right way to do things. By taking time to learn about the Aukan churches, Louis avoided the natural tendency to judge them as uncooperative by correcting his own understandings of their motivations and actions. He found that his expectations and assumptions about how they might support his translation project were totally unrealistic. Why should pastors who receive no salary at all agree to help Louis pay the salary of these young translators? Further, how could these pastors have confidence in the work of two young men who had not even demonstrated faithful service in the youth ministries of the church? By learning about the Aukan social game of church, he was forced to rethink his strategies to gain the support of these leaders for the translation project.

All the participants in multicultural teamwork must be involved in this learning process to create a community of trust. From our conversations with Pastor Waksam, Louis discovered how little the Aukan churches understood about the work of Bible translation. Accepting the fact that, as the representative of a "wealthy" development organization, he had to fund and supervise this translation project, he took time to carefully explain to these leaders why he needed to hire young men who were trilingual, educated, and technically qualified for the translation task. In these conversations together, the Aukan pastors learned that the most important way they could cooperate was to disciple these young men to become mature in their faith and to learn what it means to be "working for the Lord" in the ministry of the church. In a partnership with these church leaders, Louis directed the translation project, and Waksam and others directed the discipleship program of these young men as they worked on translation over the next decade. Through this partnership they, church and mission together, built mutual trust and completed the Aukan translation by diligent, faithful service, "working for the Lord."

Effective cross-cultural leadership cannot happen if we are unwilling to learn about and accept the social-game assumptions of our partners. We cannot negotiate effective working relationships when we have disagreements about legitimate forms of behavior and action and do not listen carefully to one another with an attitude of respect and acceptance. Further, when we allow such disagreements to reach a point where we judge and condemn one another's spirituality, we destroy any possibility of working effectively together.

The commands of Scripture make it clear that the first and most important criterion in our relationships is that we love one another. The Scriptures explain in detail how those relationships will result in patience, compassion, humility, and a host of other character attributes that flow from the work of the Holy Spirit in making us like Christ. Part of our learning to love others is to accept their decisions, as Louis did of the Aukan church leaders, even when we believe they may be poor decisions. Acceptance of this kind involves risk, yet it is foundational to building trust, which we will address in depth in the next chapter. If we do not accept others when a decision does not go our way, we lose the opportunity to dialogue about its context, about its outcomes, and about the impact that it may have in terms of the community for which it has been made. Without dialogue, we drift into the emotional trap of judging the motives of others and committing the sin of mutual condemnation. The true measure of effective leadership is whether the team does the hard work of loving one another in the midst of disagreement and then pulls together to accomplish the will and purpose of God.

5

Covenant Community,
the Highest Priority

The Strawberry Project: A Case Study

Jim served as manager of intercultural community work for a large mission operating in the highlands of New Guinea. In 1995 he returned from furlough and was looking for an opportunity to help local people improve their way of life. One day after the local farmers' market had closed, he noticed that farmers had thrown large quantities of quality strawberries into the river. He knew that these came from one nearby village, so he met with the strawberry growers to see if they were interested in finding a new market for their produce.

Excited at the prospect, they agreed to work with Jim. Jim began by drafting a marketing co-op plan and sharing this plan with the village leaders and farmers. Jim had connections in Port Moresby and arranged to fly containers of strawberries to be sold in the farmers' market and grocery stores there. The people worked with him building boxes to transport the berries, and Jim purchased individual containers to present berries for sale.

The project began with enthusiasm and great success. Jim paid the farmers for each box of berries and kept records of who delivered berries to be sold. He set the wholesale price at a level that paid for the shipping cost, direct payments to the farmers, and the cost of packaging for sale in the stores and the public market with a margin that covered contingencies. He stressed to these farmers·the need to deliver only quality berries, and he actually inspected berries during the first several months of the project.

After a time Jim's Port Moresby wholesaler reported that some boxes had rotten or bad berries in the bottom of the containers. Knowing from conversations and relationships with local people that many valued "tricking" others to see if they could get away with it, Jim was not surprised. In a meeting with the leaders, he told them that this practice was unacceptable. To assure accountability, he insisted that each farmer put his initials on the containers. When he discovered who was sending rotten berries, he refused to accept berries from these men.

Jim controlled all the money, and at the end of the first year the co-op made a substantial profit, which Jim distributed to all the participating farmers. Knowing the co-op needed to be locally owned and managed, Jim spent two years training and teaching local people how to keep the records and maintain quality. He emphasized the importance of accountability and quality control of boxes of berries received for shipping to Port Moresby. However, when he hinted at turning over the project to local leaders, people in the village resisted, and they insisted that Jim keep the money and the records.

In 1998 Jim began planning for his next yearlong furlough in the United States. He asked the village people to identify a person from the village whom they trusted to take care of the records and the money. They resisted for months, but when the day finally came when they had to make a decision, they chose two people to carry on this work. Within months after Jim's departure, the project collapsed. The local leadership, bound by a cultural norm *against* confronting those who cheat, had failed to maintain the quality of berries shipped and to manage the finances to keep the project operating at a profit (Jim Tomlinson, personal communication, 2007).

Project-Focused Leadership

This case study is an example of project-focused leadership and broken trust. The project director saw a wonderful opportunity to help people in a local Christian community create a new source of income. He discerned that the conditions were right—excellent soil and climate for growing strawberries, industrious farmers producing surplus—if only the people could get access to the urban market, which was a significant distance from their land. The obvious challenge in this project was to help the people organize as a cooperative to market their berries by air transport to Port Moresby. The project director, Jim, invested his time, energy, and leadership to organize and train these farmers in the technical skills of running a co-op and then led the implementation of this project to benefit the community.

Reflecting on Jim's leadership, we realize that he had an excellent relationship with the local people. He built friendships and trust with them so that they were good working partners. As Jim describes in the case study, he continually evaluated the process and the people. He knew these people attended church, but they didn't show Christian attitudes in their daily life and work. When those who were cheating were exposed, he, with the support of village leaders, told them that he would not buy their berries anymore. Throughout this project, Jim made numerous adjustments that were an important part of the learning of those who were contributing to the success or failure of the project, and he saw an increase in Christlike attitudes among many who participated in the project.

The question then is, why did this effort to train leaders cross-culturally fail? The first obvious issue is conflict of values: local cultural values undermined the values essential to a successful co-op organization. In that community, people accept cheating as a norm in social relationships, as long as one does not get caught. In practice, these villagers regard "getting caught" doing something that others do not like as "sin." If one does not get caught, cheating behavior is regarded as beneficial and is acceptable as long as it doesn't affect your household. The second motivating factor is self-interest and competition. Driven by self-interest, these farmers worked hard and produced surplus. Yet at the same time, they rationalized cheating that served their self-interest and thereby undermined the trust essential for the continuous operation of a cooperative. The lack of trust was the most difficult hurdle to overcome, since no one trusted anyone else with his money. Given these value conflicts and the breakdown of trust, we must ask, what is flawed in the priority for community development and better income?

The Task-Focused Priority

In his co-op training program for these farmers, Jim did not think to address the issues of self-interest and the local value for cheating or the farmers' tentative commitments to church and a new way of life called Christian. Blinded by his professional training in community development, Jim assumed that he should stick to teaching technical skills and not meddle in the local values of the culture. Jim also discovered that the organization of this co-op required some fairly complex financial management and coordination to get strawberries to market. Complexity, however, was not the problem. Rather it was the farmers' lack of trust and inability to confront clan members about poor quality berries that undermined the project. The value they placed on harmony in clan relationships and their worldview that promoted "getting my share" at the expense of others trumped the value of making money. As a consequence, Jim was not effective in raising local leadership that could manage a project of this scope. His own leadership was effective only as long as he took charge. When he left the project, the local leader who assumed his role failed.

The "strawberry project" case is just one of thousands of project-oriented ministries led by Westerners and generally focused on task. We have seen earlier in the book that these ministries often run aground because the team leader is unable to keep the team focused on the mission and goal of the work. For my purposes here, I shall refer to the "strawberry social game" orientation to ministry. Jim, as leader, tried very hard to organize the people in this local farming community to develop a fairly complex co-op focused on the production of strawberries for market. Using his development skills, he taught these farmers the roles and the rules essential for a "strawberry game" to work—a manager to direct and coordinate the routines of packaging strawberries, trucking them from the local area to the airfield, and transporting them to Port Moresby, and handling the finances of buying, selling, and paying expenses. Local leaders and farmers followed his direction until he left for a year in the United States. His departure created a crisis, and the local leaders and farmers resorted to what Jim and Ginny Tomlinson have termed their "default culture."

The Power of Default Culture

Default culture is the culture people learn from their parents and peers from birth, with all the inherent strengths and weaknesses of their society. In the strawberry case, the local farmers' lives were routinely guided by self-interest, cheating, and the accepted norm that cheating is okay unless you get caught. When the leaders and farmers defaulted to these core values, the "strawberry game" collapsed.

Jim, the project director, also operated from his default culture and professional training. American Christians often assume the separation of professional work and one's spiritual life, an expectation in their national culture. For an undertaking such as the strawberry project, Jim understood that training in technical skills was essential but did not even consider helping these nominally Christian farmers reflect on their cultural values. He organized his leadership activities and project training around his normative cultural assumptions.

The concept of default culture is essential to a clearer understanding of multicultural teamwork and the challenges of cross-cultural leadership. Every person on a multicultural team brings to the team and its relationships a default personal culture, formed during one's childhood and early development. These personal cultures have within them varying values, expectations, and definitions of roles and processes for behavior that become the default for each person when he or she faces a crisis. Although every person can learn and employ new values, social roles, and forms of organization, when people find themselves in a crisis situation, they ordinarily default to the values, roles, and ways of organizing things that they learned growing up. This default set of values provides a sense of security and order when the circumstances around them create anxiety and stress.

What is the alternative to default cultural thinking and living? Christians usually have some understanding that their new life in Christ calls them to an alternative lifestyle. In his letter to the church at Colossae, Paul reminds these young believers that the choice to follow Jesus implies dying with him in baptism and being raised with him into new perspectives and a new way of life. Paul writes, "Put to death, therefore, whatever belongs to your earthly nature" and specifically, "greed, which is idolatry" (Col. 3:5). And "do not lie to each other, since you have taken off your old self with its practices and have put on the new self, which is being renewed in knowledge in the image of its Creator" (Col. 3:9–10). Although Jim knew that these local farmers practiced both lying and greed, he only confronted them when it affected the quality of strawberries shipped to Port Moresby, and even then he did not explicitly guide these people to reflect on their new identity in Christ.

Blinded by their project focus and their default cultures, Jim and these local, nominally Christian farmers missed a wonderful opportunity to learn and practice a new life in Christ and to enjoy the benefits of that life, as a people of God on a mission for the kingdom of God. They missed the opportunity to "put on the new self," to be clothed with "compassion, kindness, humility, gentleness and patience," and to commit to God's mission and the joy of "working for the Lord."

Task versus Covenant Community Teamwork

The hidden flaw in what appeared to be a very well-designed project derives from its vision and strategic goals. As Jim describes this experience, the project began with a vision to turn strawberries floating down the river into profit for local farmers. Jim organized everything that followed around a vision for profit. What if Jim had a different vision, a vision to help these local farmers to realize their potential in Christ? What if he saw discarded strawberries as an opportunity to make disciples and envisioned their village becoming a "new creation" in Christ Jesus, a covenant community? How might this community look in two years, and what would it take to achieve such a vision?

Jim's vision defined his overall strategy and the project outcomes (see table 5.1). Given the primary goal of profit and the surplus production of strawberries on these local farm plots, Jim developed training that emphasized technical skills essential to achieve the for-profit goals. As a community developer, Jim knew that he wanted to help people with certain of their social needs. But he failed to grasp from the beginning that unless this community changed in significant ways, the social needs would not be met and the development project not sustained.

If Jim had focused the strawberry project around an agenda to create a covenant community, that goal would have demanded very different training, practices, schedules, and organization. Although the technical aspects of marketing strawberries would not change, everything else must. The vision shared with the people must focus on being a covenant community with a mission of service as followers of Jesus. Since Jim was not sure they were "followers of Jesus," he would need to take time to discuss with them what such a choice might mean, and how making such a choice would have consequences for how they sold strawberries. Whether or not they agreed to a new vision, the training must address default cultural behaviors and how "following Jesus" rather than culture in mutual relationships would change the way they worked and the rewards of working in covenant relationships. The relationships and rewards must focus on achieving the spiritual outcomes of truth and trust connected with harvesting and shipping strawberries, on compassion for fellow workers who are tempted to cheat, and on forgiveness and accountability for the next step. Finally, the profits from the project provide an opportunity for witnessing to and sharing with other villages in the area, declaring God's blessing, and giving to those in need as a way of serving Christ. Although the local people might not accept "following Jesus" and the Christian way of marketing strawberries, this type of training forces them to confront the alternatives and make a conscious choice.

Table 5.1 Task-Focused versus Covenant Community Teams

Task-Focused Team	Covenant Community Team
Goal: New income for the community	**Goal:** Covenant community
Means: "Strawberry social game"	**Means:** "Strawberry social game"
Training: Farming co-op 1. Packaging, marketing berries 2. Finance—wholesale, profit shares 3. Quality control—best berries 4. Management assuring quality	**Training:** Farming co-op 1. *Default* play vs. *Covenant* play 2. Rehearsal of the options 3. Rewards for covenant play 4. Cost of "default" play
Structure: 1. Harvest and shipping 2. Payment, financial management 3. Distribution of shares	**Structure:** 1. Truth, trust re: shipping 2. Compassion, sharing re: income 3. Witness to other communities
Outcome: 1. Expatriate-managed co-op 2. New income 3. *Default* culture destroys trust 4. Co-op bankrupt	**Outcome:** 1. *Covenant* co-op 2. "Love one another" play 3. New income for participants 4. New community leaders

The Covenant Community Alternative

Max L. Stackhouse, examining the biblical roots of the idea of "covenant" relationships, concludes that covenant for the Hebrews meant "to bind together" through the "voluntary acceptance of terms by those who are bound" (1997, 140–42). This binding together is a three-way agreement of relationship—between people and people, and between people and God. Because God plays a central role in these relationships, people become accountable to standards of moral and ethical behavior that are centered in God. Stackhouse notes that people make all kinds of deals with one another, and as we have seen in the strawberry project, they do not hesitate to cheat, manipulate, and exert power over others to advance their own self-interests. But when people covenant with one another and with God, they establish "new shared duties and rights that nourish life with other meanings, . . . established by a higher authority" (Stackhouse 1997, 140).

What then does a covenant community team look like? The apostle Peter, who had such a difficult time comprehending this in his basic training with Jesus, gives us both theological and practical direction. First, we must understand theologically the solution to this identity issue. "But you are a chosen people, a royal priesthood, a holy nation, God's special possession, that you may declare the praises of him who called you out of darkness into his wonderful light. Once you were not a people, but now you are the people of God; once you had not received mercy, but now you have received mercy" (1 Pet. 2:9–10). The transformation here is obvious: we come from vastly different backgrounds; we have identities, distorted by sin, that motivate us to hate and even kill one another; but by the mercy of God we are

1. a "chosen people" with new identity, character, and relationships, belonging to God;
2. a people on a mission "that you may declare the praises of him who called you out of darkness"; and
3. a people, once without mercy, who "have received mercy."

Every multicultural team must have this theological understanding as the foundation of its relationships. Without this understanding, their relationships are no different from those of secular or government employment, whose purpose is the power and profit goals of the employer. The key components are people with a new identity in Christ, called to the mission of God, who have received mercy and granted it to others.

Second, we must commit together to teach and practice the foundational principles of "body of Christ" or "covenant" relationships. Stackhouse notes that covenant is an intentional commitment, from the Hebrew meaning "to cut a covenant" (1997, 141). To make a covenant, then, is to form a partnership with others through a ritual meal or a ceremony witnessed by God, in which we agree together to live according to new standards of behavior founded in our relationship with God.

What are those foundational principles and how do we know? In table 5.2 I present eight core elements of biblical teaching that are foundational to practicing covenant community. Beginning with texts that reference community relationships, I have asked: How frequently is this core practice repeated in the Gospels and Epistles? And is this teaching consistent with the Hebrew Scriptures used by Jesus and the apostles to teach the first generation of the church?

Table 5.2 Principles to Teach and Practice
to Achieve Covenant Community

* Covenant Community		Text References
Identity in Christ as God's chosen people		Exod. 20:1–6; Matt. 10:32–42; John 1:10–13; 1 Cor. 1:2; Col. 3:12; 1 Pet. 1:1–2; 2:9–10
Presence of the Holy Spirit		Exod. 31:1–6; Joel 2:28–32; Luke 9:1–2; 1 Cor. 12:7–11; Gal. 3:1–5; Heb. 2:3–4
Love one another		Lev. 19:18; John 13:10; Gal. 5:13–14; 1 Pet. 1:22–23; 3:8–9
One body—serving in diversity	Servant disciples with diverse gifts as apostles, prophets, teachers, healers, helpers, administrators, etc.	Exod. 35:30–36:1; Num. 17:1–18:7; Matt. 20:25–28; 1 Cor. 12:27–31; Eph. 4:1–16
One body—working together in unity	Respect, honor, and equal concern for every member	Jer. 32:38–40; Ezek. 11:19; John 17:20–23; 1 Cor. 12:21–26; 1 Thess. 5:12
Submitting to one another	Affecting all relationships: no one is excepted	Matt. 16:24–26; Gal. 5:13–15; Eph. 5:21; 1 Pet. 2:13–17; 3:8–12; 5:5
Speaking graciously	Do not judge, condemn, or spread false witness; rather, edify and encourage	Exod. 23:1–9; Matt. 7:1–12; 1 Cor. 4:1–5; James 4:11–12
Restoring mercifully	Forgiving and restoring those who sin	Deut. 4:31; 15:7–10; Mic. 6:8; Luke 6:27–38; Gal. 6:1–3; Col. 3:12–14; 1 Pet. 3:10–11

The first core principle is that of our new identity in Christ. The struggle for people in multicultural teams derives from the attachment they have to national, local, and family identities that have shaped them from infancy. The Gospels and Epistles tell the stories of God calling and redeeming a people for himself through the work of his son, Jesus Christ. This new identity has profound implications for us—called by God, holy, dearly loved—and also is an invitation to a life that begins by denying self, taking up our cross, and following Jesus. As such this new identity supercedes all other identities that we have and must be the conceptual frame through which we relate to all people. Our loyalty to clan, community, and nation must take second place to our identity with Christ and with the people of God.

Second, as Gerhard Lohfink notes, our identity as the people of God stands upon the presence of the Holy Spirit and the manifestation of the power of the Holy Spirit through the community of believers (1984, 81–87). From the moment when Jesus sent out the Twelve (Luke 9:1–2), he gave them power through the Holy Spirit to carry out the work he commanded them to do. Without the power of the Holy Spirit, multicultural teamwork is just another task-focused group of people trying to do a technical job. Lohfink notes, "Where Jesus spoke of the reign of God, the early church spoke of the presence of the Spirit. . . . Signs and wonders belong to the essence of the New Testament communities. . . . When God's salvation became present, disease and possession had to yield" (1984, 86). A team that has no clear manifestation of the presence of the Holy Spirit must question whether it has a legitimate call from God for mission.

The third principle, loving one another, flows from our identity as the people of God and the validating presence of the Holy Spirit. Jesus states, "By this everyone will know that you are my disciples, if you love one another" (John 13:34). Love is the defining character of the people of God living in covenant community. At the same time, we may legitimately ask, what does a community of love look like? Does everyone agree with one another all the time? Certainly this was not and cannot be the case. The other principles help us to see more clearly what a loving community looks like.

The metaphor that Paul gives to this loving community is the "body" of Christ. And within this community all members have a distinctive calling; Jesus made it clear that disciples are first and foremost servants who know their master's will and are faithful until he comes (Luke 12:41–48). Paul defines this servant calling with reference to the diversity of gifts given by God to those servants—apostles, prophets, teachers, healers, helpers, administrators, and so on—who then work together in unity, without placing one gift in higher regard than another. The "body" is characterized by its inclusiveness; all the members are essential, and although we think some are "weaker" or "less honorable" than others, "God has put the body together, giving greater honor to the parts that lack it, so that there should be no division in the body" (1 Cor. 12:24–25).

Lohfink suggests that we experience the "arrival of a new world of God in Christ" in which God eliminates the social barriers endemic to societies and brings Christians together into a reconciled community (1984, 93). We are to work together in unity, giving respect and honor to and showing equal concern for every member. Paul speaks often of the "building up of the community" and the "*responsibility which all in the community have for one another*" (Lohfink 1984, 102, emphasis his). The fact that God loves and honors the weak and less significant among us should motivate us to do the same. Those who work with their hands are as honorable as those who teach or administer, and those who are less able, less productive, or handicapped mentally or physically must be given a place and treated with honor and respect.

To assure that we love one another as Christ has loved us, the Scriptures give us clear and practical instructions about our relationships with one another (table 5.2). We are to "submit" to one another in Christ, and there are no exceptions. First Peter 2, 3, and 5 give clear and detailed instructions about submission to one another as the people of God and to our unbelieving neighbors and rulers. Within the community of faith, Peter tells us to submit as is appropriate within the culture, younger to elder (5:5), wives to husbands (3:1–5), husbands to wives (3:7), and then counter to culture, everyone should submit to one another (3:8; 5:5–6). To those in the wider community—rulers, neighbors, masters (employers)—Peter says, "Submit yourselves for the Lord's sake" (2:13). Other texts are even more specific. Paul tells us in Philippians that we must "in humility value others above" ourselves (2:3). He goes on to say that we should give priority to the "interests of the others" (2:4). Jesus sums it up with the challenge repeated in all the Gospels: "Those who want to be my disciples must deny themselves and take up their cross and follow me" (Matt. 16:24).

Finally, we must obey Christ's commands that are core to covenant relationships—"do not judge" (Matt. 7:1–7) and "be merciful" and "forgive" (Luke 6:35–37). Judgment and condemnation are absolutely destructive to covenant community. Dallas Willard shows how judgment and condemnation destroy relationships and undermine every kind of ministry (1998, 217–24). Willard argues that we must develop loving communication with one another, communication that begins with the "ask," seeking to understand the thoughts and motives of a sister or a brother in Christ. Without this commitment to ask, listen to, and love one's neighbor, covenant relationship cannot happen.

All of this is impossible apart from the grace of God and the power of the Holy Spirit working in our teams and communities. As people with responsibility for leadership, we must continually humble ourselves before God, acknowledge our powerlessness apart from God, and seek to be channels for the Holy Spirit in this work of equipping and leading a team. We must also pray for the gifts of mercy and forgiveness, essential to rebuilding relationships when, for whatever reason, they are broken. Paul challenges us to "bear with each other and forgive one another if any of you has a grievance against someone. Forgive as the Lord forgave you" (Col. 3:13). Covenant relationships are impossible without forgiveness. People are first of all emotional creatures. Although we like to think we behave rationally, when someone challenges our will, we respond with emotions of anger and revenge. Our natural inclination is to return evil for evil, insult for insult, injury for injury. For this reason the Scriptures challenge us repeatedly to overcome evil with good (Rom. 12:17–21; 1 Pet. 3:9–14). Praying as a community for the grace of God to bestow a spirit of mercy and forgiveness and then practicing together the disciplines of mercy and forgiveness enables us to fulfill the commandment to love one another.

The Essential Priority: A Community of Trust

The strawberry project provided a powerful story to remind us that the thousands of project-focused ministries in mission have at their core misplaced priorities. Although some might want to lay this burden wholly on Western, materialist cultures, the problem lies deeper in our human character and spirit. People in every culture learn early that work is essential to life, and that individual or group achievements confer recognition and benefits to the participants. Task focus is not Western; it is a value shared by people everywhere, illustrated well by our case study of villagers from the New Guinea highlands.

The story also helps us understand how much human behavior is driven by what I have called default cultural values. People learn patterns and priorities of work, sharing, self-interest, competition, and conflict as children, and form habits for life while growing up in their families and communities. We have seen how adults can and do learn many new ways of relating to others as well as skills for work and relationship. Yet in situations of stress, people default to those habits and behaviors acquired early in their life experience, habits of the "flesh" rather than habits of the "spirit."

In this chapter I have argued that leaders and followers must reverse the order of their priorities. Instead of giving first priority to attaining vision, meeting goals, and productivity, they must rather give highest priority to the formation of a community of trust and then to doing the hard "bodywork" of creating both community and trust. Leaders must help the group center on their new identity in Christ and lead them in a process of commitment to Christ and to one another to be the people of God on mission together. The ideas of covenant community and covenant commitments provide both theological and sociological frameworks for cementing a team's commitment to God and to the other members of the team.

Finally, leaders and followers must be willing to commit to the training and practice that leads to covenant community teamwork. We have seen in the strawberry project case study that technical training was essential to achieve the project goals and that covenant community training, which was not done, could have provided the essential relationships, values, and behaviors to make the project a success. The next chapter outlines some of the practical team-building and training strategies essential to creating covenant community teamwork.

6

Creating Covenant Community

What Makes a Ministry Team? A Case Study

Sue Kim is a second-generation Korean American serving on the pastoral staff of a large Korean American church in Los Angeles. One of her responsibilities is to train the young people to learn more about cross-cultural issues so that they can function more effectively both in the United States and in other countries. After listening to the youth, she learned that most of the young people dislike the African Americans they encounter in the city, primarily because they just don't understand them. To help Korean American youth learn what missions is all about, each summer the church sponsors young people for short-term mission trips to two or three different countries.

In the summer of 2006, Sue worked with the youth ministry leaders of the church to plan a training program for Korean youth who would be going on a two-week ministry trip to the Masai people in Kenya. A Korean missionary in Kenya working with the Masai was their contact and local ministry person.

When asked what kind of training they used to prepare these students for the summer trips, Sue reported that they met for eight hours every Saturday for twelve weeks prior to the missions trip. "What did you do during that time?" I inquired. "Well," she replied, "the pastor talked about the importance of prayer; then I preached for about one hour from the Scriptures; then several Saturdays we had missionaries come in and tell us what they had learned from the countries where they served. We also watched two videos."

As I reflected on her report, I realized that at the end of twelve weeks the leaders had no understanding of what these young people had learned, and they had done nothing beyond preaching and praying to help these young men and women become a missional community. The young people had gained no practical experience for learning how to connect to people in another culture or for serving the Masai that they would visit in Kenya. Sue said she would have liked to use more simulation exercises, but the senior pastor insisted they should focus on knowing the Bible and spending time in prayer, so that is what they did.

Worship—The Pledge of Covenant Relationship

The Korean pastor had the right instincts but the wrong application when he insisted that the youth mission training focus on Scripture and prayer. As we noted in the previous chapter, covenant community is a partnership between people and God, framed in the voluntary submission of people to work together for the mission of God, under the lordship of Jesus Christ. These covenant relationships must be formed in worship—an experience of the people of God, submitting to God and to one another in a public commitment to holiness, unity, and mission. Max Stackhouse notes that in the Hebrew context that commitment usually involved people sharing a meal together, an animal sacrificed to God and then eaten together in worship, fellowship, and commitment (1997, 141). As part of worship, people heard the Scriptures and committed, in the presence of God, to obey them as the people of God.

The Korean pastor's error lay in his limitation of training to the practice of preaching and prayer. David Watson states, "God's people are called to be a worshipping community. Having come to Jesus, that 'living stone,' Christians are to be like 'living stones built into a spiritual house . . . to offer spiritual sacrifices acceptable to God through Jesus Christ'" (1978, 179–83). Watson goes on to speak of worship as sacrifice—of our bodies, of our possessions, and of praise. It is this kind of sacrificial worship that Stackhouse describes as binding people and God together in covenant community relationships.

If we think back to the strawberry project in chapter 5, the Christian villagers in the highlands of New Guinea never thought of their farming enterprise in relationship to God and had not even imagined that God might have an interest in how they farmed, sold their berries in the market, or worked together in a co-op. People cannot begin to imagine the sacrifices required of covenant community relationships apart from their worship of God. Unless training begins in worship, the teaching of holiness, love, and sacrifice makes no sense. It is only in the context of the Holy God that people begin to take seriously the teachings of Scripture about our bodies as "living sacrifices" (Rom. 12:1) and about our possessions as something to be shared with others (Heb. 13:16).

Leaders who wish to create covenant communities must make worship an intentional part of the experience that people share in community. That worship must focus on God as the source of all that we are and have as human beings. Further, God in Christ is the one from whom we receive grace and forgiveness, and the one who calls us to a new life of holiness and grace in him. This worship experience must be communal, involving teaching, fellowship, food, and prayer (Acts 2:42–47) and should include a time of personal and communal commitment to practice, by the grace of God, the principles of covenant relationship outlined in chapter 5. As Stackhouse has noted, the sacrificial meal was central to covenant relationships for the Hebrews (1997, 141); for Christians the meal and rite of commitment must include the Eucharist, sharing the bread and the wine to remember the profound love of God toward us and to give thanks for the mystery of salvation and the gift of new life through the death and resurrection of Jesus Christ on our behalf. "If we are truly committed to one another and are willing to lay down our lives for one another however painful this may be, the life of the risen Christ will be manifested among us" (Watson 1978, 244).

Learning—Through Preaching or Practice?

In the case study of Sue and her pastor, we see a commitment to teaching Scripture and prayer, but no evidence of any consideration of youth committing to covenant relationships, learning the practice of ministry, or reflecting on the default culture that they bring to serving others. In the case study of the strawberry project in chapter 5, we found strong emphasis on technical training for marketing and running a co-op, but no consideration of default culture or of covenant community commitments. Both of these training programs have fatal flaws, each neglecting one or more of the critical variables essential to covenant community teamwork.

Training for a covenant community team must lead participants to understand the difference between how one behaves in one's default culture and how one behaves in a covenant community. Simply put, training must engage participants in such a way that they learn how "practicing ministry" from a default culture mode is very different from "practicing ministry" in a covenant community mode. This kind of training takes longer and is much more difficult than technical or "preaching" training, requiring simulation, reflection, and repetition for learning, *and the work of the Holy Spirit* to transform the motivation and actions of participants into covenant relationships.

For example, a Korean elder, supervising the short-term ministry of youth in his church, stated, "We must have and teach rules for our teams, so that someone doesn't play music at 2:00 in the morning." I challenged him that "rules" do not teach team members how to obey Christ and live in covenant community, but the alternative is more complex. To teach youth how to love one another requires simulation that contrasts default cultural behavior and covenant community behavior, and then discussion about what is pleasing to Christ. I suggested an example simulation: five young people are sleeping on the floor; one gets up and begins to play the guitar and sing at 2:00 a.m.; the others wake up and start shouting at the "musician"; an argument ensues, and the young guitarist continues playing in spite of the conflict. The leader then guides the youth through a debriefing: "Put yourself in the place of these five. How would you feel? Who was right, wrong, and why? How do you think these young people would act if they had covenanted together to submit to one another in Christ?" Then ask them to create two or three new simulations. What would this 2:00 a.m. scene look like if we were trying to practice Philippians 2:1–5, and esteem others better than ourselves?

Training for Covenant Community Teamwork

As we have seen in the strawberry co-op case study in chapter 5, the default culture mode of the local New Guinea community accepts that cheating is the norm, getting caught is a sin, and self-interest is the primary driver for human behavior. Before these Christian farmers begin thinking about producing strawberries and shipping them to market, they need to experience, practice, and discuss how covenant community differs from their default culture. The trainer must design careful training exercises that allow them to experience and compare the differences between default cultural and covenant community ways of doing things. People must role-play and rehearse the options. They must understand the outcomes of the default culture play—cheating, getting caught, or not getting caught—and self-interest. These exercises should include options in which the players cheat successfully and unsuccessfully with the consequences of each. Then they must learn, practice, and prayerfully reflect on covenant play and default play and the consequences of each. "Covenant play" gives priority to the interest of others (Phil. 2:1–5), looks at one's brother as an essential partner for one's success, and teaches the value of caring about one's brother as much as one cares about oneself.

Training for covenant community teamwork requires the kind of careful simulation that enables people to see that over the long term, forsaking God's way leads to bitterness and frustration (Jer. 2:19). Simulations 1 and 2 in sidebar 6.1 illustrate the kind of training exercises necessary to help people engage these issues. Building on the strawberry co-op case study, simulation 1 is designed to have participants play out the cheating option in selling strawberries. The motivation is good: to get enough money to pay school fees for one's children. The situation is common: good and bad berries, and not enough to earn the money needed. The dilemma for "me," the actor, is how to get the money I need. The simulation develops the choice of cheating and the gain and cost of cheating for the individual and the whole group.

Simulation 2 creates an alternative set of choices that focus on covenant relationships. The need and the farmer's dilemma are the

Sidebar 6.1 Simulating "Default" and "Covenant" Play in New Guinea

Simulation 1: Default Culture Play

1. I need $25 for children's school fees (25 boxes of strawberries).
2. My harvest yields 20 boxes of good berries, 7 boxes of bad berries.
3. I empty 5 good boxes and fill 10 boxes—half bad, half good berries.
4. Truck pickup—I sell 25 boxes (10 with bad berries), $1 each, $25.
5. Market in Port Moresby sells 400 boxes of berries at $2.50 each, but has 10 angry customers who return their boxes and demand a refund. The merchant charges the co-op $4 for each returned box of berries.
6. The director asks whose name is on those boxes. When he finds out they are my boxes, he tells me he will not buy my berries for four weeks. My neighbors are angry when they learn they have each lost $2 from their share of profit because of the returned boxes.
7. Debrief: What did I gain by cheating? What did I lose? What did my neighbors lose because I cheated? Did I feel ashamed? How did this situation hurt or help the co-op as a community?

Simulation 2: Covenant Community Play

1. I need $25 for children's school fees (25 boxes of strawberries).
2. My harvest yields 20 boxes of good berries, 7 boxes of bad berries.
3. I take my 20 good boxes to pickup and tell my story to neighbors. Out of compassion, 5 neighbors each give me 1 box of berries to sell.
4. Truck pickup—I sell 25 boxes, $1 each, $25.
5. Market in Port Moresby sells 395 boxes of good berries at $2.50.
6. The director tells us that the merchant in Port Moresby was very pleased with the berries, and we have earned $5.94 in co-op shares for each farmer.
7. Debrief: What did I gain by asking for help? What did I lose? What did my neighbors lose by helping me? What did they gain by helping me? How did we feel about the good news from Port Moresby? How did this situation hurt or help the co-op as a community?

same, but he lives in a community that is working to learn how to love one another. This is the test: does the farmer have the courage to ask for help, and will his neighbors give him the additional five boxes of good berries that he needs? If they act in this way, what are the economic consequences and the effect on community? The key to these simulations is debriefing at the end of each. The participants must discuss the economic, social, and moral consequences of each set of choices.

The economic consequences of each scenario are summed up in table 6.1. Employing default cultural values, the "cheater" does gain the extra $5 needed for his children's school fees, but the co-op loses $40 (about $2 a share) in returned berries and merchant costs. Further, the cheater loses the opportunity to sell berries for the next four weeks. The long-term economic cost of cheating is actually rather severe in this simulation.

In the "covenant play" option, the farmer who humbles himself and asks for help gets the money he needs for school fees, and five of his neighbors sacrifice one box of berries, $1 each, to help him. The economic outcome of these choices is actually better for all of them. The farmer who asked for help can continue to sell berries over the next four weeks, and he makes $2 more in co-op profit than he would have gained by cheating. Those who sacrificed $1 for their neighbor gain $2 in co-op profit, offsetting their gift.

Table 6.1 Economic Outcomes of Simulations 1 and 2

	1. Default	2. Covenant
Income		
Gross	$1,000.00	$987.50
No. of boxes	400	395
Expenses		
Farmers	$400.00	$395.00
Shipping	$300.00	$300.00
Merchant	$200.00	$197.50
Return charge	$40.00	—
Co-op profit	$60.00	$95.00
Share	$3.75	$5.94

Debriefing: Learning from Reflection, Repetition

The essence of simulation training lies in the power of reflection and repetition. The leader must guide participants in debriefing discussions that explore the personal, communal, and moral consequences of these choices. Participants in the strawberry project must discover for themselves that in the short term, the default value of cheating often provides a benefit, but in the long term it always undermines the character and well-being of the community. And they need to reflect on God's Word about these actions and the cost of disobeying God. By discussing anger, shame, and other emotions, they may contrast the impact of default and covenant play with regard to shame, positive self-image, peace, and better economic well-being for all the participants.

Chris Flanders suggests that taking time to worship God, in the midst of debriefing, "may be a place where these activities can be brought into the lives and identity-shaping work of the Holy Spirit" (personal communication, 2007). This suggestion brings us back to a fundamental principle of covenant community: God is witness to our commitments, the source of the grace that enables us to follow Jesus, and the spring of the living water of love and forgiveness that enables us to accept and forgive others (Col. 3:12–16). Short periods of worship in debriefing sessions may help participants to reflect on the presence of God in the discussion and on our utter dependence on God for the solutions we forge in our reflections. By acknowledging the presence of God in the debriefing process, we allow the Holy Spirit more time to speak to participants and to lead them to critique their default cultural patterns and focus their conversations on covenant behavior, such as loving one's neighbor.

Covenant community play must be designed specifically for each culture and local community. We cannot employ stock training modules and programs or use standard curriculum. To effectively create such a training program, the leaders of the project must begin with careful study of the local culture and understand exactly what default culture play looks like. Only then, from a careful understanding of the local cultural values, can the contrast between default culture play and covenant community play be simulated. My wife, Judy, and I have as our next writing project a book that addresses how to design and teach for these covenant community learning outcomes.

Outcomes of Covenant Community Teamwork

The primary outcome sought for covenant community training and teamwork is the shift of the team's focus *from* its "project game" *to* being a covenant community in Christ on mission. If the training is effective, the team will take steps toward being a transformed Christian community *in the midst of* organizing and mobilizing people to accomplish a "project game" with specific goals and objectives. In the strawberry farming case in New Guinea, the local people would learn through the training process what it means to be a covenant community playing the "strawberry marketing game."

The outcome of this training should result in an understanding and practice of what I would call "love one another" play. The participants in this process will have examined the costs of playing the self-interest game of the default culture and have some understanding that in the long term default play will destroy the project. They will also begin to understand that if they play the "love one another" covenant community way, in the long term they may benefit in new and significant ways.

If the training program is in fact effective, and if participants willingly participate in the covenant community teamwork, the outcome will certainly be new income for participants in the strawberry game. Further, in the training process individuals will emerge who show potential to lead this game once the project trainer is gone. The objective of covenant community teamwork is that people will in fact become successful in leading themselves, and their projects will thrive through their leadership.

Does covenant community teamwork ensure that a project will succeed? No. In spite of their best efforts to follow Christ, Christians usually drift back into default cultural play, and as a consequence their efforts to work together fail. I cannot guarantee that the kind of training I have outlined here will in fact produce new income or whatever other results the participants in the teamwork desire. But such training and focus will certainly change the basic foundations upon which people work together. As people engage the Word of God, as they think about how it defines their relationships and roles together, and as they begin to attempt to simulate and practice working together using these kingdom values, many of them will surely follow Christ. When people follow Christ, new and different things happen. The world in which they live and work is changed by the impact of their faithfulness and by their example.

So, whether the strawberry project succeeds is not quite so important. What one hopes in a project such as this is that the people who have studied carefully what it means to be a covenant community will emerge as more faithful disciples of the Lord Jesus Christ. As faithful disciples, they will have learned how to live together in the ways defined in Scripture as the body of Christ. If this happens even to a modest degree, God will be honored, and people and communities will have embarked on the journey of being transformed by the renewing of their minds in Christ Jesus (Rom. 12:2).

7

Trustworthy Leadership

Divided and Discontented: A Case Study

A small team of four (two Thais, an American, and a Canadian) work together to alleviate poverty in an arid, hilly area of Southeast Asia. Tawat's father is a high-ranking general from the elite of Thailand. During his university days, Tawat met a Christian exchange student who shared the gospel with him, and through his witness, Tawat converted to Christ. Eight years ago, Tawat joined the team and has been a faithful and loyal team member, yet the value he places on hierarchy has created significant tensions for the North Americans on the team. The expatriate team leader, Brian, has expressed frustration that Tawat has continually vetoed the acceptance of new Thai members onto the team. Tawat, in contrast, finds Brian very naive: "Brian thinks that just any Thai can join this team. If we aren't careful, they will want to have equal decision-making power with us, who have been together for a long time, and that's not right, because they don't know anything yet. My leader needs to learn wisdom and act more slowly."

In Thailand there is a sharp dichotomy between those of high rank, who have power, and those of inferior status, who do not. The power distance between Thais has led to repeated conflict over decision making on this team. The conflict has grown so tense that one or another member of the team often cancels or postpones the weekly meetings. The discontented partners say that the team meetings are too long, and both sides have become entrenched in their position as they argue.

The team leader, Brian, has confided that while he is fond of his team members, he is so frustrated at their unwillingness to compromise that he often acts unilaterally. He has given several examples of situations where he had secretly carried out ministry activities in ways that were contrary to the ideals of his teammates. The clashing values between team members has led to stagnation, secrecy, and failure to achieve their goals (adapted from Dierck 2007, 126–27).

Power Distance and Conflicts about Decision Making

The D-Team case study represents all the things that one should not do when leading cross-culturally. As we look at the details of the case, it is clear that the focus of this team is project—not covenant community—teamwork. The participants are dysfunctional as a team, and because they cannot make decisions or work together, they also have had marginal success at creating income-generating projects.

Brian has not addressed the cultural differences among team members or given priority to forming covenant relationships within D-Team. It is clear that the senior Thai member on the team has blocked Brian from recruiting new members and has used his own personal default culture as the guiding framework for his relationships with the other team members. He has rejected the team leader's culture, does not see value in the team leader's objectives, and does not support decisions contrary to his preference or interest.

Reflecting on the perspective of Robert Banks and Bernice Ledbetter (2004, 18)—namely, that leadership enables a team to translate vision and values into action—we see that the team leader, Brian, has first completely failed to align his people with the vision that was the basis for forming the team or to achieve any practical project implementation. Brian, the "leader," acts autonomously, not consulting his team members in order to get something done. It is clear that Brian is not leading; he is just doing his own thing.

Second, Brian has failed to find an interest in or to incorporate any intentional way to create covenant community relationships among members of the team. Although they have in common the fact that they are believers in Jesus Christ and wish to engage in a Christ-honoring ministry, they have done nothing to address issues of trust and to treat one another as vital members in the body of Christ. They are unable to resolve their cultural differences because they have not committed to building the spiritual relationships of mutual love and trust essential to working together.

Third, Brian and the team have not recognized their fundamental differences regarding power and hierarchy, and they have failed to negotiate a social game that they can all agree upon for the conduct of their work. Until they define the attributes of relationship and power that will characterize their teamwork and agree to commit to these principles, they can never work as a team. Lorraine Dierck notes that the decision making in D-Team is so tense that individual members cancel or postpone meetings and complain that meetings are too long, and others are inflexible. They also lack a sense of covenant commitment to one another.

Citing Geert Hofstede (2001), Dierck attributes these behaviors to different understandings among them about power and power distance. The Thai members of D-Team have a default culture that places every person into a hierarchy of superior and inferior positions. Tawat holds a view that Hofstede calls "high power distance," in which the gap in the hierarchy between leader and follower is very wide, so wide that followers have no access to the decision-making process (2007, 91). The North Americans reject hierarchy and default to individualism and equity. The gap between the Thais and the North Americans is so wide that they have little hope for working together. Unless they acknowledge their differences and then covenant to act with respect toward one another, they will never be able to construct the rules of a social game for the team that bridges their cultural differences. To achieve such a compromise, both must relinquish aspects of their default cultural bias as they work toward covenant community teamwork.

The members of D-Team have fallen into the dysfunctional pattern of seeking to control the team agenda and refusing to grant power to others. They want things to happen according to their default priorities and interests and refuse to esteem other members of the team better than themselves. In short, this is not a team. It is merely an association of individuals who have decided that they will try to work together for community development projects. Although they have been able to obtain funding for some of the things that they want to do, they do not have the ability to work together or to mobilize others to work with them to accomplish their projects. The leader is not leading, the team is not following, and there is no effective multicultural teamwork in this context.

False Identities That Undermine Trust

The members of D-Team seem incapable of applying the principles of their faith to their team relationships. If they have ever tried, they have lost the capacity to listen to one another, to love one another, and to forgive one another. Regretfully, this deafness to the principles of Scripture is common in Christian ministries. Careful examination of Scripture illustrates repeatedly how people cannot hear a God who challenges their experience and way of life. The disciples in the very presence of Christ did not comprehend much of what he taught them. The stories of Peter in the Gospels provide numerous examples. Although God reveals to Peter that Jesus is the Christ (Matt. 16:16–17), Peter completely misunderstands the meaning. Imagining that Jesus will be a triumphant king, Peter rejects outright Jesus's explanation of how he will suffer and die at the hands of the rulers and priests. Jesus tells him bluntly that his interpretation is from Satan (Matt. 16:23). A short time later James and John induce their mother to ask Jesus to give them the seats on his right and left when he comes into his kingdom. Jesus asks them, "Can you drink the cup I am going to drink?" They imagine the goblet of a king, as they confidently assert, "We can" (Matt. 20:22). In fact, however, they are deluded, having no understanding of his message to them.

We may be quite confident that we are not as blind as the disciples, but that arrogance frequently increases our blindness and leads us to great disobedience. The case study of D-Team illustrates how much we see others and ourselves in the light of our own values and self-justification. The tragedy of multicultural ministry is the ethnocentric agendas that the participants bring to these admirable attempts to be the body of Christ.

At the heart of our blindness and ethnocentrism is a false perception of our identities and significance. The political wars of the twentieth century have left a deep seed of conflict in the global church—the leaven of "nationalism" as a core feature of our personal identities. This is an ancient deception (Jew or Greek, free or slave, Scythian or barbarian) that has taken on new clothes in the twentieth century. In Europe, the Americas, and Asia, two world wars and the cold war have produced societies in which nationalist identities have become dominant features of human relationships. In a recent meeting with Chinese Christian leaders at Fuller Theological Seminary, I heard the chairperson of the China Christian Council declare that Chinese Christians must be good patriots, and that they must reconstruct theology so that they have a distinctly Chinese theology for the church. As I pondered these statements, it suddenly occurred to me that her motivating vision was nearly identical to the vision of many US church leaders in the twentieth century—an anticommunist, anti-Islam, Republican, pro-American, "the world left behind" theology of Christianity.

How do we help people called to ministry refocus their identities from being American, Korean, Singaporean, Australian, or Kenyan to being first and foremost Christians, followers of Jesus Christ? Paul challenges the Galatians directly on this point: "There is neither Jew nor Greek, neither slave nor free, neither male nor female, for you are all one in Christ Jesus" (Gal. 3:26–29). Until believers grasp fully who they are in Christ, they will not be able to "serve one another humbly in love" (Gal. 5:13). Our honorable efforts to create mission-focused multicultural teams are aborted by this deception of global politics and the enemies of Christ.

Contested Social Games of Decision Making

In addition to issues of power and power distance, members of D-Team have very different expectations about decision making. In chapter 4 we saw how Louis and Pastor Waksam in Suriname had different social-game assumptions about ministry work and leadership. Louis learned that he had to work through the Aukan church social game to win the local churches' trust and develop effective partnership and leadership for the translation project. In Lorraine Dierck's (2007) study of six multicultural teams (composed of members from three or more nationalities) in Thailand, she found differing social-game issues present in all of them. Figure 7.1 presents a summary analysis of these six teams. I have called four of those teams D-Teams, since they are divided and discontented and their members are struggling over different social-game preferences, as we saw in the case study of D-Team that opened the chapter. I have labeled the other two C-Team (corporate) and E-Team (egalitarian), since they have each adopted a social game, albeit different ones, for decision making and teamwork.

Figure 7.1 Social Games of Thailand Multicultural Teams

Bureaucratic Game	GRID +	Corporate Game
		C-Team—corporate
		D-Teams—divided
− GROUP		GROUP +
Individualist Game	GRID −	Collectivist Game
		D-Teams—divided
		E-Team—egalitarian and consensus

C-Team, comprised of eight Thais and two expatriates, had a corporate social structure led by four senior members, each having an area of specialized responsibility. C-Team worked effectively together, doing evangelism and leadership training. The Thai emphasis on hierarchy and group discussion provided the framework for decisions and teamwork, and members embraced this without dissent.

E-Team, comprised of four Thais and seven expatriates from two Western nations, operated from an egalitarian, consensus–decision model. The team had very lively discussions about development and evangelism, shared their views openly, and used a "yes" vote to affirm decisions individually. Dierck noted that E-Team avoided "against" votes on proposals, because such a process would cause loss of face for Thais and the whole team. The expatriate leader consciously stayed away from team meetings to promote greater participation by Thais and an egalitarian consensus for team decisions.

The other four D-Teams experienced varying degrees of disagreement about the decision-making process and at times dysfunction in their relationships and teamwork. Three of these teams had clearly defined leaders or leadership teams, but members often spent hours discussing an issue, and then unhappy team members often lobbied quietly against the resulting decision, eventually forcing a new team meeting.

Dierck observed that Westerners on these teams tended to press for collectivist leadership values, and the Thais, while less forceful, persisted with hierarchical assumptions and corporate values. An expatriate mission director giving oversight to another all-Thai ministry team adamantly opposed Thai corporate culture:

> I prefer to keep the decision-making as flat as possible in my organization. Decisions must be made at the lowest level. We must challenge the hierarchical style of leadership in this country. I have had a few Thai team leaders, and I hate the way they throw their weight around. It caused a lot of problems on the team. I address that by teaching about servant leadership. To me, servant leadership means that anyone who has a vision should be empowered to start a new team and a new ministry. My job as leader is to help people fulfill the dreams they have in their heart. (Dierck 2007, 115)

In spite of this mission director's opposition to the Thai social game of leadership, on the all-Thai team under his direction one woman provided very effective corporate leadership for her team, following Thai values.

We can observe from Dierck's research that disagreement about the appropriate social game of leadership on a team can and does have a negative impact on the capacity of team members to serve together effectively as the body of Christ. C-Team and E-Team demonstrated consensus, although different kinds, on the social game of work and leadership that they followed. They worked with unity and purpose to accomplish their ministry goals, having a positive impact for the people they served. The four D-Teams (divided and discontented)

could not reach consensus on the critical issues of how to make decisions and who should lead. The Thais and the expatriates on these
teams disagreed about how to organize and do the work, and rather
than discuss and agree on an appropriate social game of work, they
judged one another and condemned their teammates for failing to
understand "servant leadership."

The failure of the D-Teams can be traced directly to their lack of commitment to covenant relationship. On the positive side, Dierck reports
that some expatriates and Thais on these teams did respect one another
and surrendered their preferred ways of doing things to a broader team
consensus. On the negative side, more team members clung adamantly
to the idea that they held the superior and "biblical" view of teamwork
and leadership. Expatriates on these teams widely shared the critical
viewpoint of the Western mission director about Thai hierarchy. Yet
the data show that when members surrendered their preferences, they
could work quite effectively, employing a modified version of Thai
hierarchy. It is this surrender of preference, or one's cultural bias, that
represents the essence of a servant to the body of Christ.

Surrender of preference is not always, or even often, a meeting-in-
the-middle compromise. Sometimes it is more appropriate to adopt
"Thai hierarchy" or some other local cultural form of organization.
Louis, in the case of the Aukan church in chapter 4, understood that
he had to accept the Aukan social game to achieve legitimacy for his
translation team; a middle-road compromise would not achieve that
goal. In multicultural teamwork surrender is more complex, as we see
from the four D-Teams in Dierck's research. Surrender might mean
commitment to a new structure that is different for all the participants
or to an organizational framework that participants agree together
is most effective for the mission and vision. The key to surrender is
covenant relationships—people united together to fulfill their shared
mission as the body of Christ.

Leadership for Impact

The D-Team case studies illustrate how individuals who hold tenaciously to their national and social-game values, certain that their way

is God's will for their team, undermine any potential for covenant community and produce minimal results. Max DePree in *Leadership Is an Art* (2004) suggests that leadership is not achieved through structures or social processes. Rather, leadership is how one lives within a structure, respecting the people, accepting their differences, and engaging them in ways that inspire trust and transform yet sustain relationships and structure.

I am indebted to Max DePree, who spent his career in corporate business, for the insight that effective teamwork begins with a leader's commitment to covenant community. DePree challenges leaders to see their people as participants in covenant community, committing to one another as people, agreeing to support one another. Reflecting on the D-Team case study that opens the chapter, DePree would argue that Brian has the duty as team leader to love the people whom God has brought to his team and to help them build covenant relationships with one another. This is particularly critical on multicultural teams. People come together with different national identities, cultural histories, and values about work and leadership. Unless they dialogue together about these differences and covenant to give their identities in Christ priority in their relationships, it will be impossible for them to work together. Dialogue toward covenant relationships is the most important and the first work of a team; without it a "team" does not exist.

Yet a covenant relationship is not one that lacks accountability or focus on productivity and results. A team member must be accountable, and a good leader will let a person know when he or she falls short, and provide guidance on how to improve. Again reflecting on D-Team in Thailand, we realize that Tawat has repeatedly obstructed the addition of new Thai members to the team. Brian has not taken time to learn why and to challenge Tawat with the mission and covenant of the group. Likewise other members refuse to attend meetings and avoid the tough process of making decisions together. Brian has neglected the hard work of leadership by his own confession. He has simply acted on his own, breaking whatever covenant the team had to work together. Brian must show his commitment to team members and at the same time hold them accountable for their commitment to one another and to their mission.

DePree would agree that effective teamwork is not about democracy and/or consensus. Leaders make decisions for the good of the team, the well-being of its people, and the effectiveness or results of its ministry. But such leadership need not be power focused or governed by the tyranny of consensus. Rather, a leader defines the rules of participation to reflect inclusiveness in the body of Christ, commitment to the work of the kingdom, and effective communication among team members that understands the essence of mutual submission, weakness, and forgiveness. This kind of leadership is not driven by results but rather is focused on mobilizing people to concentrate on mission and work effectively together to achieve the very best impact for the corporation or the ministry.

Biblical "Form" or Biblical "Leadership"?

The expatriate mission director, who adamantly opposed Thai corporate culture, expressed certainty that his vision of "servant leadership" was the correct biblical "form" that must replace the distortions of Thai cultural leadership. He used his role and resources to drive the team members toward his "transforming" form of empowerment and decision making. Such leadership behavior distorts and destroys the very teamwork and community relationships that the leader aspires to achieve.

This distortion resides first in the assumption that there is only one kind of servant leadership: that which is expressed in an individualist, egalitarian vision of social life. Most of the Westerners on these Thai multicultural teams have embraced the individualist, egalitarian vision and define servant leadership in terms that fit their social values. They are free to do what they "feel called" to do and to "fulfill their dreams." They do not bring to the table a commitment to relationship over self-fulfillment or a willingness to submit to others with a priority for unity. They do not see building trust in covenant community as a greater priority than their ministry focus and calling. They assume that "exercising my gifts," and "doing ministry tasks" are more important than "being the body of Christ."

Leading multicultural teams or leading in partnership with national churches creates greater complexity and requires higher commitment to the principle that we must "be the church" to fulfill the mission of God. To be the church is to become a covenant community as outlined in chapter 5, loving one another, committed to mutual trust, and obeying Jesus Christ in all that he taught about "following" and being his disciples.

As Dierck has shown in her research on multicultural ministry teams in Thailand, division undermines trust in nearly every team, limiting God and mission by a default culture that we have sanctified as the "our spirit revealed" social game. Mission becomes "our vision," finance is for "our strategy," controls are to assure "our outcomes," and accountability is to assure "our standard of quality." The illusion that seduces all leaders and followers is that we have the "right form" for God's work, and we trust the form and system rather than God. Leaders become power seekers, rather than servants in the work of the Master, the mission of God.

In conclusion, the critical factors for leading cross-culturally are Christ-centered learning and trustworthy covenant-centered leadership. In my previous books I have argued that cross-cultural ministry requires a commitment to entering into a culture, beginning as a learner. I have shown how Jesus in his incarnation lived among the people for thirty years, learning first the rules of family, community, work, and worship before he began to proclaim the gospel of the kingdom. I have argued that even as Jesus, who was fully God, became fully human, we must move out of our nationalistic cultures and values; enter into the family, community, work, and worship world of the people we hope to serve; and become like them. We can never fully identify with them, but we can relinquish those aspects of our values and culture that cause pain for others and take on those aspects of their culture and values that create mutual trust and commitment. In effect, we learn to be less "us" and more "other," perhaps adding enough to our cultural repertoire to become 150 percent persons, retaining 75 percent of the values and patterns from our culture of origin and adding 75 percent of the values and patterns from the other culture (Lingenfelter 2003, 24–25).

However, it is clear to me now that the 150 percent–person model is inadequate for much of the multicultural teamwork happening in mission in 2007 and beyond. For example, in Wycliffe International the work of Bible translation often involves team members from four, six, or more cultures. In such a situation, participants cannot hope to learn the cultures of all team members well enough to adapt to and live in their home communities. So what can we do? Max DePree has guided us to the kind of leadership essential for teamwork—extraordinary leadership that builds trust through covenant relationships, inclusiveness, and commitment to obey Christ and to communication among team members until we achieve the unity of the Spirit and love that leads to forgiveness and oneness of purpose and action.

Part 3

Pathways to Empower

8

Power-Giving Leadership

To Control or to Concede? A Case Study

In the first three years of his ministry, Pastor David sought to implement a program of radical change in his church, launching new programs and bringing in new associates to lead them. He did not seek advice from anyone in his congregation but relied on his own insights as to how this congregation might experience revival and growth. His personal ambition, fueled by his perception of the expectations of the search committee who appointed him, became the driving force of his ministry.

At first the elders of the congregation supported his leadership, but gradually David's forceful leadership style began to alienate them. David believed that a good leader exercised strong control over the direction and implementation of ministry in his church. And during his first year of ministry, his predecessor told him, "If you want to be effective, and accomplish the vision God has given you, you must lead with an iron hand. The elders will oppose you, but you must challenge them forcefully."

Pastor David viewed his elders as enemies, people who would block his ministry and renewal in the church. As a consequence, even though at heart he was a gentle person, he created conflict and opposition in his relationships with his lay leaders. The tension in his ministry ultimately exhausted him emotionally and spiritually. And this congregation proved much more difficult than his first pastorate. His wife and children also suffered from the constant pressure.

David also struggled to build a new pastoral team. One of his earliest decisions was to release the three men who had served the previous pastor as associates. He met with them shortly after he took office and informed them that they needed to begin immediately seeking other appointments. However, he would not fire them but would give them time to find a new position. Although one found a position in the first year, the other two hung on for three years until they were able to move. During this time they found it very hard to work enthusiastically for David. And building teamwork in the congregation was nearly impossible.

In the fourth year of his ministry, with his new associates now in place, David planned a fall retreat for prayer and renewal of vision for the ministries of the church. The day before the participants' planned departure, a severe storm poured heavy rains and snow that made travel to the mountain retreat center extremely precarious. A group of women elders came to David and asked him if they could hold the retreat at the church instead of at the mountain setting. Indignant that these women would be bold enough to question his plan, David's initial reaction was to reject it. Yet, in listening to his people over the past year, he had sensed that his leadership created more pain than progress, and he personally longed for more peaceful relationships with his elders.

As he debated internally the dilemma of appearing weak versus making a foolish decision to force his people out on a potentially treacherous journey, he could not reach a decision. He saw clearly the danger of forcing his plan, yet he dreaded the thought of weakening his leadership authority. Further, giving in to the women elders seemed a greater weakness than conceding to the men. Wracked by his fears and indecision, he turned to seek direction from the Lord. As he prayed, the Holy Spirit urged him to trust God and to trust his people. He was reminded of the Scripture—he who seeks to save his life will lose it, and he who loses his life for my sake will find it. He decided to concede to the request of these women.

The impact of his decision to accept the counsel of his women elders was profound. First, the men and women expressed their gratitude and renewed excitement about the retreat. Then, through prayer, worship, and seeking direction from God, pastors and elders for the first time began to listen carefully to one another. At the end of the retreat, pastors and elders felt a new sense of trust for one another and a readiness to move forward together in ministry.

To his amazement, David found that his concession to the women elders had actually strengthened his leadership. After the retreat, all the elders seemed more committed to him and to his vision. These reactions forced him to struggle inwardly with his philosophy of leadership. How much should he listen? When is compromise more important than clarity of direction? How is God leading, and why and how will people follow? Out of this experience he resolved to alter his leadership so that he listened more to his elders and associates and worked with them to construct a unified vision and direction of ministry.

Power as Control

Control is the basis of power. People who seek to control their circumstances, their jobs, their relationships with others, and their effectiveness in their work are all seeking power. Pastor David, like most people, did not like to think of himself as engaged in power relationships with others. We, like him, prefer to reflect on and describe our activities as motivated by an interest in quality, the desire to assure that things will be done well, to protect those who are unable to protect themselves, or to fulfill our responsibilities. Such activities are not understood as being power-seeking or power-exercising activities. Yet, as Pastor David illustrated well, such actions at their core are intended to control the outcomes of an event in accord with the interests of the person retaining control.

Marguerite Shuster, focusing on the human psyche and power as a dimension of personal identity and action, defines power as "the ability to produce intended effects in the world" (1987, 156–57). As soon as a child is old enough to understand that communication produces intended effects, the child will seek power in his or her relationships. Shuster suggests that a person's existence becomes linked to the kinds of things that one produces. Some find significance in work, others in the multiplicity of relationships, and still others in wealth. A person who does not find his or her life leading to at least one significant end feels impotent and even hopeless. Shuster also suggests that Pastor David and all the rest of us find our meaning and existence linked in a large degree to our sense of power to exert our wills in our world.

Richard Adams takes a social and economic approach to power (1975, 9–20). He contends that people have power to the extent that they control elements of the environment, material or immaterial, sought by others. Adams argues that power differences are an inherent characteristic of all social relationships. For example, in the opening case study, Pastor David controlled the jobs of his three associates; he controlled the location, the content, and the schedule of the retreat that he required his men and women elders to attend; and he controlled the decision process and outcomes for his elders and staff.

Control of the environment occurs in all ministry activities. A church or mission employer controls the amount and kind of work and the compensation that an employee is given for his or her labor; the Bible "translator" controls the choice of text, the exegesis of meaning, and the compensation for a national-language "helper" working on a Bible translation. In each of these relationships, one person controls concrete aspects of the environment that are valued by others. Adams suggests that "power transactions" are those reciprocal exchanges between persons of unequal power that result in each obtaining some measure of self-interest.

Both Adams and Shuster help us to understand that power has significant implications for one's identity as a person and for one's interest as one engages in social relationships. Pastor David was terribly anxious that a concession to the women in his church would ruin his reputation as a leader and destroy his ministry. Our natural inclination is to seek power to assure that we have meaning and significance in our lives. Further, our personal interests motivate us to engage in reciprocal exchanges with others that satisfy our mutual interests and our need to control events to achieve desired ends.

Power Exchanges and Will

If Adams is right and all social relationships have embedded within them power distinctions, then the normal course of social life results in numerous power exchanges. A *power exchange* occurs when someone who controls something of importance to another uses that control to obtain compliance or conformity of the other to his or her will. For example, Pastor David used his power to fire the three associates of the former pastor, while giving them time to find other positions. Often these exchanges are so routine that people do not recognize the implicit issues of control. For example, a pastor tells the music leader the topic of his sermon and assumes that the music leader will select songs that support the topic. The music leader tells the worship team and the organist/pianist what music will be sung and played in the service on the next Sunday and expects them to be prepared to perform as instructed. In each of these relationships, one person controls some aspect of the environment that is of significance to the others. Although the musicians control their skills and performance, the pastor decides what content and even perhaps which selections will be performed. If the music leader rejects the pastor's guidance, the pastor may withdraw support for the music leader and act to remove that person from the worship team. And so it is with each of the other relationships. The structuring of power relationships as Adams describes them is a normal part of the social structure of society. We can hardly avoid these power differentials, nor should we try to do so. They are an essential part of how we work together in society.

While Adams is correct in his assessment of the inherent material basis of power relationships, Shuster helps us to understand that our exercise of power in these relationships ultimately focuses on an aspect of our inner person, our will (1987, 94–95). All people bring will to bear on their relationships with one another. Our will emerges from inner motives, often from our personal need to seek power or to avoid impotence. The case study of Pastor David reveals a man fearful that he will lose his power to lead.

Shuster suggests that evil is a result of "*disruptions of structure and/or will*—the Devil spoiling what God has made" (1987, 140). These disruptions lead people to distort the structures of human relationship.

and exercise their personal will in the pursuit of power. Perversion of
the structures of relationship most often comes from our obsession to
achieve a particular good, such as a biblically sound church. In view of
that good, we may construct false paths (keeping control in our hands)
to achieve the desired end and make our way the absolute and only
way to that end. As we saw clearly in the case study of Pastor David,
when we accept the deception of sin and pursue a good in the wrong
way, the end is misery both for us and for the people we seek to serve.
The disruptions of will flow from our choices of lesser goods (e.g.,
my vision for ministry instead of obedience to God), rigid adherence
to our worldview, and blindness to and rejection of others.

Each of these distortions—perversion of structure, false paths,
lesser goods, rigidity—leads us into destructive patterns of behavior
and relationship. When our will is thwarted, as in the case of Pastor
David, we seek to punish others and reassert our control. In our arrogance, we limit options to those we know and opt for choices we
believe are secure, rather than take the risks that obedience to God
demands.

What Is Power-Giving Leadership?

Following Shuster's understanding, I will first argue that *we must
put Jesus "in the place of power as a proper source of healing and
will"* (1987, 209, emphasis mine). We must understand that power
cannot be the source of our meaning and significance if we are to be
the people of God and leaders who follow Christ. Shuster suggests
that "giving fallen humanity power only magnifies their potential for
wickedness" (1987, 201). Human structures become tyrannical, human
will becomes self-serving, and the quest for power leads people to all
kinds of temptation and evil.

To restore our human psyche and relationships to the will and
purpose of God, *Jesus must become the center of who we are and
replace our quest for power.* Only as we are motivated by the Holy
Spirit and through the living Word of God can we relate to one another
within the structures of human society to accomplish the purpose
of God. Yet Shuster notes that it is impossible for us alone to make

the radical changes that would have the Word replace the quest for power in our lives (1987, 202). The only possible way that this can occur is through the grace of the Lord Jesus Christ. Pastor David found this grace as he prayed for direction from the Holy Spirit in his difficult decision to yield. It is precisely this grace and focus on the life-changing power of the Holy Spirit and the transforming power of Jesus, the Living Word, that enables us to shift from power-seeking to power-giving leadership.

Walter Wright identifies the second essential principle: *power-giving leadership is in its essence relational, rather than positional* (2000, 2, emphasis mine). Instead of focusing on authority and responsibility, the Christian leader works to build relationships that influence others to follow Christ. Jesus demonstrated such leadership, investing his life in a few unlikely disciples, challenging them with his vision of the kingdom of God, and thereby transforming their Jewish world and culture. Jesus became their friend and mentor; he visited their workplaces and families; he invited them to join him in proclaiming good news and healing to the broken. The fruit of the Spirit in his life modeled service *to others* and values that challenged the cultural establishment with its power-seeking leadership.

The centrality of relationship means that *people are more important than authority and control*. This then affects the kind of exchanges that take place between leaders and followers. In the typical power exchange, the leader exercises control in such a way that the will of the leader is done, often at significant cost to the follower. One of my colleagues tells the story of how his mission leader demanded that he do exactly what the leader instructed and that he do it without question, even at the cost of his personal integrity. In this pattern, the follower is servant, and the leader is served. Wright suggests that relational leadership reverses this exchange, and the leader is servant, seeking the "growth and nurture of the followers" (2000, 13). *Instead of powering outcomes, the relational leader builds trust and influences followers through integrity of character and depth of relationship.* Pastor David discovered, to his astonishment, that his decision to yield to the women elders transformed his relationships with the men and women elders of his church and greatly enhanced his leadership among them.

In the pages that follow I present several essential practices for mission and church leaders that place Jesus in the position of power and give relationship priority over authority and control. Contextual leadership is premised on the acceptance and empowerment of others. To achieve contextual leadership, the missionary, who so often controls resources and knowledge, must intentionally surrender control and trust Jesus to accomplish his purpose in those he has called to ministry. When we obey his command to love first, relationship takes priority over control, and contextual leadership becomes possible.

Paul, Philemon, and Power-Giving Leadership

The letter of Paul to Philemon in the New Testament provides one of the few fully developed case studies of a relationship between a leader and one of his followers in the New Testament. This relationship is also a cross-cultural relationship. Paul, as we know, was a very devout Jew, and early in his career he rejected anything associated with the Gentiles. After his dramatic conversion documented in the book of Acts, Paul became an advocate for Gentiles and a zealous missionary proclaiming the good news of Jesus Christ to urban Greeks.

From the text in Philemon, we know that Philemon was a wealthy Greek slaveowner from the city of Colossae in Asia Minor (Col. 4:7–9) and the leader of a church that met in his home. Paul has many good things to say about Philemon. He calls him a "friend and fellow worker" (Philem. 1). He commends him for his faith and "love for all of God's people" (v. 5). Philemon was apparently also a significant leader in his own right in the church community. Paul comments that in his service Philemon "refreshed the hearts of God's people" (v. 7).

To understand Paul's leadership, it is important to recognize his current situation and status in life. Paul is a prisoner in Rome, so when he introduces himself as "a prisoner of Christ Jesus" (v. 1) he is speaking both figuratively of his relationship with Christ and literally of his current condition under house arrest in Rome. Paul also calls himself "an old man" (v. 9), and in the story he appeals to Philemon as a younger "partner" (v. 17) in ministry.

The crux and dilemma of this story is that Onesimus is a runaway slave belonging to Philemon. Although it is uncertain how Onesimus and Paul established a relationship, the letter makes clear that this runaway slave has become a deep, personal friend of the apostle. As Paul writes to Philemon, he says that Onesimus "became my son . . . in chains" (v. 10). Paul has deep affection for this man, and from the letter it seems evident that Onesimus has cared compassionately for Paul in his imprisonment and perhaps failing health. However, by the legal standards of Roman society, Paul should return Onesimus to his master, who owns him and has the freedom to punish him in whatever way he deems appropriate. For Paul this creates both social and spiritual dilemmas.

The spiritual dilemma seems more critical to Paul. He can deal with the social problem by reminding Philemon of his significant debt to Paul, but the spiritual issue cannot be resolved so easily. The fact is that two brothers in the Lord, Philemon the master and Onesimus the slave, both apparently converts of the apostle, are not reconciled with each other. Further, Paul has deep friendships with both men. In his grief at this discovery, Paul realizes that he cannot rest until he has taken steps to bring about their reconciliation.

The power of this letter lies in Paul's candid description of his emotions and his struggle with his own selfish desires. He openly declares, "I appeal to you for my son Onesimus," who was formerly "useless to you, but now he has become useful both to you and to me" (vv. 10–11). Table 8.1 summarizes Paul's words as he reflects on the choices that are open to him. In one set of options, he talks about how he could use the power available to him to get what he wants. For example, Paul says, "I could be bold and order" (v. 8). He goes on to say, "I would have liked to keep him . . . so that he could take your place in helping me" (v. 13), and concludes, "He is very dear to me" (v. 16). In all of these expressions, Paul is identifying his own emotional attachment to Onesimus and the sense of obligation that he feels Philemon has toward him. He recognizes that he has the power just to tell Philemon to forget it and forgive Onesimus and leave him with Paul.

Table 8.1 Paul's Power-Seeking or Power-Giving Options

Power-Seeking Option	Power-Giving Option
• I could order, v. 8	• Your consent, v. 14
• I want to keep him . . . so he can help in your place, v. 13	• Separated that you might have him back for good, v. 15
• He is very dear to me, v. 16	• Dearer as a fellowman and brother, v. 16

But Paul does not follow through with his own selfish motivations. Instead he takes the power-giving as opposed to the power-seeking option. He states, "I did not want to do anything without your consent" (v. 14), and he notes that he would prefer Philemon to act spontaneously and not out of coercion. As Paul reflects on the relationship between Philemon and Onesimus, he surely must consider the possibility that Philemon will not return Onesimus to him. Onesimus is still a slave, the property of his friend Philemon. In his former service he was apparently a useless slave, behaving badly, and then running away. As Paul reflects on this, he concludes that possibly Onesimus should return to Philemon and make good all those bad years in which Philemon has endured the useless servant. At the same time Paul emphasizes that Onesimus is, at this point, better than a slave; he is a dear brother in Christ. And so he encourages Philemon to receive this transformed slave as someone who has become dearer, "both as a fellow man and as a brother in the Lord" (v. 16).

A dramatic moment in this text occurs in verse 8, when Paul engages in what Dallas Willard (1998) calls the "ask, seek, and knock." Although Paul could make some assumptions about how Philemon might respond, and he could try to argue with Philemon about those possible responses, he instead asks Philemon to extend grace. Paul begins by pleading, "I appeal to you on the basis of love" (v. 8 NIV), love for "an old man" and "also a prisoner of Christ Jesus" (v. 9). He then moves directly to the main question of his letter: "I appeal to you for my son Onesimus, who became my son while I was in chains" (v. 10).

I confess that the language that Paul uses here has often irritated me, even to the point of thinking Paul was being petty and almost coercive in his relationship with Philemon. Even though he states that he does not want to do anything without Philemon's consent, he uses language that places tremendous emotional pressure on Philemon to return Onesimus—"you owe me your very self" (v. 18), or "confident of your obedience," or "knowing that you will do even more than I ask" (v. 21). Paul is reminding Philemon of some deep obligations to Paul, and I have interpreted Paul's words as leverage to get Onesimus back.

But after reflecting on this text again, I am inclined to be a bit more gracious in my judgment of Paul's action. In spite of Paul's words, one key fact cannot be denied. Paul sent Onesimus back. This was a very painful act for him, and yet he did it. His pain is evident in his words, such as "you owe me" (v. 19) or "I do wish . . . some benefit" (v. 20). The critical fact of this letter is that Paul released his control over Onesimus. He had control, he could have kept control, but he gave it up.

In those days of travel on foot and by ship, the separation that Paul endured because of this decision was not a trivial matter. The journey for Onesimus from Rome to Colossae in Asia Minor involved no less than two or more months' journey on land and sea. Under these circumstances, Paul might never see Onesimus again. To release Onesimus to go to Philemon was, in fact, to say, "I might never see him again."

Power-Seeking versus Power-Giving Leadership

Paul's actions in this letter illustrate, in a profound way, the difference between power-seeking and power-giving leadership. Christopher Flanders (personal communication, 2006) notes:

1. The very existence of the letter tells us that (a) it was a serious matter for Paul, and (b) there was a good chance that Paul's requests might go unheeded. Otherwise, the letter makes no sense if it was simply a "slam dunk" kind of request. This highlights the difficult and challenging nature of power-giving leadership, even for an apostle of Christ such as Paul.
2. Leadership always occurs within a context of pressures and expectations, which in this case included a letter read in public;

Paul's intended visit; the theological rationale for Onesimus's return; the precedence of Philemon's character.
3. We must consider other possible outcomes. Wasn't Paul within his "rights" to keep Onesimus? How could Paul have rationalized such a move? What would be the implications of doing such?

The power-seeking leader is preoccupied with control. The power-seeking leader uses control to assure the "best" outcome and releases control over resources only when he or she is certain of the intended outcome. If Paul had exercised power-seeking leadership, he would have kept his control over Onesimus, a significant resource person to both Paul and Philemon. For Paul that benefit included service and companionship. For Philemon that benefit included the return of a lost investment, the resumption of service as a slave, and/or punishment of a runaway to protect his reputation as a man of wealth and standing in the community. Each man certainly struggled with internal desires to secure his investments in this young man.

The power-seeking leader uses position and authority to exert mastery over others. In this situation, Paul used a letter to engage in a power exchange with Philemon. He had Onesimus in his custody, and he could have easily written a different letter that would have asserted Philemon's obligations to him and induced Philemon to release Onesimus to Paul without ever letting Onesimus out of his sight. Paul understood that if he took that tactic, it would be a false path to acquire something that he desired. He would pervert the relationship that God had given him with Philemon, using his position as the senior brother in Christ to advance his own selfish interest. In doing this, Paul would have, in fact, undermined Philemon's faith and the work of the grace of God in their relationship together.

By returning Onesimus to Philemon, Paul refused to retain the immediate benefit of Onesimus's company and service in hopes of the greater benefit of reconciliation between a master and a slave. Paul understood that reconciliation could not happen until Philemon and Onesimus met face-to-face. Philemon and Onesimus must confront each other, and Onesimus must ask for forgiveness for his sins against his master, Philemon. Without this personal encounter, any form of reconciliation would be incomplete.

Empowering for the Mission of God

How does this case study contribute to the focus of this book, leading cross-culturally? To reflect again on the definition, leading cross-culturally is inspiring people who come from two or more cultural traditions to participate with you in *building a community of trust*, and then to follow you and *be empowered by you to achieve a compelling vision of faith*. The case study of Paul and Philemon focuses on two fundamental issues of our definition: building a community of trust and empowering others to achieve a compelling vision of faith.

Paul chose to follow God's will in this matter and place reconciliation and restoration of trust between Philemon and Onesimus as the very first priority. By sending Onesimus back, Paul surrendered control over their relationship to the power of God and to the will of each man to be reconciled to each other. Through this significant act, Paul granted both Philemon and Onesimus true freedom.

Flanders suggests that power-giving leadership can occur only with the willing participation of others in the relational equation (personal communication, 2006). The story makes it clear that Onesimus sought freedom and risked running away to achieve it. His return to Philemon placed everything he had sought in jeopardy. If Paul had forced Onesimus to return, that would have been another form of power seeking. The text infers that Onesimus willingly returned, reflecting his new identity in Christ and a desire for reconciliation. Paul sought to persuade Philemon to also become a willing partner in this reconciliation. Flanders notes, "Giving Philemon the freedom to choose is also a vision to grow ('I know you'll do even more than I ask'). Part of empowering leadership is to remind people of who they are and the way their (potential) actions are consistent with their identity in the Lord" (personal communication, 2006). Paul's words to Philemon emphasize his duty in the Lord to both Onesimus and to Paul, and by fulfilling this duty freely, Philemon will grow in his own power-giving leadership.

But perhaps even more important, Paul is always focused on the mission of God. His desire is that the gospel of Jesus Christ be proclaimed, and that believers be faithful in their witness to Christ by word and deed. He reminds Philemon at the beginning of the letter, "I pray that you may be active in sharing your faith, so that you will have a full understanding of every good thing we have in Christ" (Philem. 6 NIV). Tom Wright highlights Paul's focus on partnership, correctly noting that fellowship has less to do with warm feelings and personal affection and more to do with coordinated activity in shared life together (2004, 198). Wright explains that he is "praying the partnership which he and Philemon share in the gospel will be productive, will have the effect it's meant to" (2004, 200). Paul's passion is larger than his relationship with both men; he desires the personal reconciliation in Christ that embodies the very nature of the gospel.

Flanders suggests that the story is about "meaning making," Paul framing these events into divinely inspired, redemptive relationships and identities (personal communication, 2006). To pick up the themes of chapters 5 and 6, Paul is teaching Philemon and Onesimus what it means to live out covenant community in Christ. Flanders cites Markus Barth and Helmut Blanke, who argue that "the name 'Onesimus'" is equivalent to the Greek term for "'bad,' 'wicked,' 'shameful,' 'painful,'" and that this letter creates a new identity for him, a slave who has been redeemed, set free, and empowered to willingly return to his former master and submit to his authority and wishes (Barth and Blanke 2000, 339). Further, Flanders notes, the metaphors that Paul uses for himself—"mother, friend, partner, prisoner, old man—all explicitly de-emphasize structural authority and power." Flanders concludes, "This is not necessary when leaders rely on structural power. Those given to raw use of power do not have to justify or explain their power moves. To give power assumes that leaders provide other rationale, explanation, and motivation that frame the issues and requests. This Paul does masterfully throughout the letter" (personal communication, 2006).

Through this story Paul illustrates the attitudes essential for power-giving leaders. When leaders follow the command of the Lord to love one another and to esteem others better than themselves, that obedience changes the nature of all human social interactions, including those of leadership. We have no assurance in this or any other text that Onesimus was, in fact, able to return to Paul. The story is incomplete. We don't know if Philemon and Onesimus were reconciled to each other. All of that is left in the hands of God. We do know that Paul chose to relinquish the power he had in order to seek the reconciliation of these two men and offer a more compelling witness of the transforming power of the gospel to everyone who knew them. This is power-giving leadership.

In the chapters that follow we will explore pathways to empower others to take up the burden and responsibilities of leadership. Chapter 9 focuses on how to mentor broken young people like Onesimus and take the essential steps to empower and release them for ministry. Chapter 10 examines the question of how one can give away power and still produce the necessary and intended results of ministry. Chapter 11 asks how leaders can effectively exercise power, which they must do, and yet avoid the traps of power-seeking leadership.

9

Empowering and Mentoring

Mentoring from Weakness: A Case Study

A few years ago the director of a European mission gave a young missionary named Gerald the responsibility of leading several community churches on a Pacific island. The mission had worked in these islands for thirty years, and a series of earlier missionaries had planted churches, translated the Bible into the vernacular, and established regular programs of worship, Sunday school, adult Bible studies, and youth ministry. Gerald and his wife had come to the islands to direct the youth ministries and had done that successfully for four years. When his senior missionary colleague left on extended furlough, the supervision of the local mission and its diverse ministries fell to Gerald, including preaching each Sunday and training national leaders to continue the work.

Gerald found the weekly preaching particularly difficult, for he was still struggling to learn the local language and was decidedly less gifted in language than the colleague who had preceded him in this ministry. As he pondered how best to minister to these local churches, he prayed and asked God to lead him to men who could assist him in the ministry of preaching. Stepping out in faith, he asked a few of the local men in these congregations for assistance.

Over the next year, Gerald developed relationships with several men as they served as his interpreters. One man, Joshua, had an alcohol problem and was struggling in Christ to be free. Gerald and Joshua agreed to work together, each knowing they could not go on without the other. They agreed to call each other "fifty-fifty," knowing that neither could do the work alone. Gerald would prepare his weekly sermon in English and then meet with Joshua on Saturday to review the sermon. Together they discussed the meaning and implications of each aspect of the message. Through such conversations, Gerald and Joshua prepared their messages for Sunday morning worship services.

As these two men worked together over the next three years, Joshua gained increasing skill in understanding the text and translating the messages into the local language. As they discussed the Scriptures, they found illustrations to apply each text to the life of people in the island congregations. One day Gerald asked Joshua if it was necessary for him to give the message in English. He suggested that they continue to prepare the text together, develop illustrations, and have an appropriate outline and application for the sermon, but that Joshua preach the message without an obvious missionary presence. Joshua agreed but was quite nervous about preaching alone.

When Sunday morning came, they prayed together for the power of the Spirit to guide Joshua in delivering God's Word. With renewed courage, Joshua delivered his first solo sermon so effectively that the people in the congregation expressed their joy and appreciation. From that time on, Gerald assisted Joshua and others in these local congregations to prepare Sunday messages, and gradually he stepped aside as the Holy Spirit led them to be the "up-front" leaders in the worship services. By the time that Gerald left for furlough three years later, Joshua was witnessing to his family, ordering Christian books, and studying more and more of the Bible.

What Gerald had seen as a weakness, his lack of language fluency to preach, had actually become a strength. When his colleague had left the church four years earlier, there were no local men capable of preaching in his absence. When Gerald left at the end of the four years of his leadership, Joshua had become a faithful and effective leader and preacher, and four other local men were equipped to effectively study, teach, and preach the Word of God.

Empowering the Impotent

The focus of power-giving leadership is to follow Christ and, in so doing, to lead others to follow Christ. In the patterns of "normal" cultural life, our power and skills may produce leaders but probably won't produce followers of Christ. People will certainly imitate us, and if we effectively demonstrate our skills and act to produce socially desired outcomes, they will do the same. The effect, however, is disastrous for the kingdom of God. The history of the church is littered with the tragic stories of powerful leaders who not only failed to bring about the kingdom by force but caused great damage to the church.

In the case study above, Gerald illustrates how to lead out of a position of weakness. Assessing clearly his own giftedness, he recognized that he was unable to carry on the kind of ministry that had been the pattern of his predecessors. At the same time, he also understood the importance of leading these island people to follow Christ. Although he was anxious about his ability to do so, in his weakness he succeeded in training and empowering local church leaders to conduct the ministries of the church.

One cannot raise and empower leaders without creating opportunities for them to lead. Alan Weaver in his study of church leaders in Hungary noted that every leader who mobilized others did so by creating opportunities for them to lead within their congregations (2004, 149–53). These men understood that unless they created roles and new ministry opportunities, their training of leaders to lead was flawed at the outset. When Gerald surveyed his congregation to discern to whom God might be speaking and then invited several to join him in this venture of the weekly preaching ministry, he created new ministry opportunities.

One obstacle that people often cite in arguing not to empower others is that these others lack qualification. Some use this argument as an excuse for retaining control and refusing to turn ministries over to others. In fact, very few people are qualified in the beginning for service in the kingdom of God. Gerald discerned correctly that the most important qualification was the calling of Christ in the life of a person. In the case study of Gerald and Joshua, previous missionaries had rejected Joshua as unqualified. Joshua had a problem with alcohol, a common problem in these islands that disqualifies many people from serving in ministry. However, Gerald saw that Joshua did not want to be the prisoner of alcohol. As they worked together, God gave Joshua victory over the alcohol abuse, and Joshua became an effective preacher and leader in his local congregation.

What are the essential qualifications for the work of ministry? Every kind of ministry requires certain mental and technical skills. However, we often give these skills higher priority than they deserve. The most important qualifications involve one's commitment to Christ, their intention to continue growing in spiritual life and character, and the willingness to use the gifts that God has given to the person, gifts that can be nurtured for the particular ministry in mind. When God calls a person and provides the appropriate giftedness, that person may achieve the essential skills through mentoring and training.

One of the most important principles of empowerment is to release people to do the work, always within a context of discipling them, and at the same time to resist the temptation to intervene to assure the correct results. Gerald illustrates this principle in his equipping and mentoring of Joshua. In the beginning they prepared the message together; then Gerald preached and Joshua translated. As Joshua's study and preaching skills improved, Gerald observed that Joshua, although he lacked confidence, was able to prepare and preach effectively without him. When that day came, he released him to study, prepare messages, and set his own course, but he did not withdraw his support as mentor.

The most important part of empowering new leaders is to support them in the early stages when they need help and to release them as soon as they can walk in the ministry by themselves. Consider the analogy of a toddler learning to walk: as soon as the child takes steps alone, we encourage the child to keep going. Some people are very cautious about releasing young leaders; this is a serious mistake. To release is not to abandon but to let the young leader learn to walk. It is vitally important that we allow young leaders to take halting steps, allow them to stumble, even fall, and then, as mentors, encourage them to get up and try again. We can always support them and help lift them up after they have fallen. But they will never be successful leaders unless we release them to play the game, to do the work for which we have equipped them.

Mentoring Missional Leaders

The case study of Gerald and Joshua shows that Joshua became effective because Gerald carefully mentored him over an extended period before releasing him to ministry. This mentoring required Gerald to spend significant personal time with Joshua. Mentoring involves much more than just training people to preach sermons or to translate Scripture or to perform some other task. Mentoring engages the mentor and the disciples in an ongoing personal relationship that helps each of them to grow deeper in his or her walk with Christ.

The mentor must see his or her role as servant of Christ, participating in the life of the new leader in a way that strengthens and builds that person up as a follower of Christ. This requires the mentor to ask questions about any alcohol problem, about personal disciplines in walking with Christ, about sexual behavior, and about the areas in which the disciple may be struggling. At the same time, the mentor must be a source of encouragement, never of condemnation. Mentors who condemn and judge their followers will never be effective in raising them up as leaders.

A mentor who is discipling the young woman or man to be a leader in a community must understand that listening, learning, and empathizing is the first step, but the second is speaking truth in love. The mentor must help the younger leader in the same way that Christ helped his disciples. Jesus did not hesitate to confront Peter when his values were contrary to the gospel of the kingdom. Jesus did not hesitate to confront James and John about their ambitions to be first. It is essential that a mentor confront the disciple by speaking truth and helping that person grow in her or his walk with the Lord Jesus Christ.

Mentoring for mission is the most important aspect of this process, but unfortunately we too often focus on programs rather than mission. The case study of Gerald and Joshua illustrates a program-focused ministry—Gerald inherited worship, Sunday school, adult Bible studies, and youth ministry programs, and the responsibility to keep them going. His mentor and mission director expected Gerald to nurture and grow a form of church framed in the Reformation that emphasizes preaching on Sunday as the method of making disciples of the people of God. When Gerald had completely transferred preaching responsibility to these local island leaders, he had achieved a very important transition in this ministry, equipping local leaders to teach and preach. But Joshua and these other men had not yet acquired a vision for mobilizing their people for the mission of God.

From the perspectives developed in this book, Gerald's program-focused mission reproduced churches and people who proclaimed what Darrell Guder calls a "benefits salvation" gospel (2000, 120), a reduction of the gospel and the church to what they can do for their members. Gerald and his mission leaders focused on building local worshiping communities, yet these communities lacked a sense of vision and mission within and beyond the island community. Although Gerald grasped the basic principles of reproducing leaders, these leaders became effective teaching and worship leaders for an expatriate model church. We do not see in the case study that Gerald encouraged Joshua to mentor others to teach and preach, as he had been mentored. Without a compelling vision to reproduce leaders on mission, Joshua did not replicate Gerald's mentoring, and the island churches continued the program-focused pattern of the Reformation churches of Gerald's home community.

Mentoring to Manage or to Lead?

The challenge of equipping new leaders is to decide whether we will mentor them or manage them. When we focus on managing, we are intent on controlling the ministry to be sure that things happen in the way we want them to happen. Robert Banks and Bernice Ledbetter note that managing is a process whereby we seek to bring consistency to our work and processes (2004, 18). Managing new leaders then means that we keep them focused on the results that we desire, we control the resources that we give them so that they do things the way we want them to, and we generally channel their work toward the specific goals that we have in mind. The result of this kind of mentoring is that we produce not leaders but rather people who serve us, working to achieve the objectives that we have defined for our purposes.

Management is essential to all complex organizations, and I do not wish to suggest that management itself is in any way wrong. However, mentoring for management is not mentoring for leadership. If we in fact want to produce leaders who can work in multicultural contexts and bring teams together to focus on the work of the kingdom of God, then we must mentor them to be leaders and not simply the people who will implement our plans.

Again in the case study of Gerald and Joshua, we find Gerald's focus on managing the operations of the mission and the church. Faithful to his training, Gerald understood his work as a missionary to be managing the services of the local church, supervising the upkeep of the mission and church property, overseeing the programs for youth and children, and training local leaders to do the same. Gerald served faithfully and effectively to carry out this agenda, and he did it well. Joshua learned from Gerald how to do the same things—but this is not a compelling vision and does not fulfill what we understand to be the mission of God.

Mentors Release Control

If we aspire to develop new leaders, then we need a different focus—a focus on the mission of God and following Jesus to make disciples of the nations. This is an immense vision and defies mere management strategies. Banks and Ledbetter suggest that "leadership activity is aligning people" by translating vision and values "into understandable and attainable acts" (2004, 18). Working from this perspective, we see that the essence of leading is to help people align their gifts and energies for mission, and then, once they understand the action required, to release them to do the work.

Jesus illustrates this focus and process. When he sent out the Twelve, "he gave them power and authority to drive out all demons and to cure diseases, and he sent them out to proclaim the kingdom of God and to heal the sick" (Luke 9:1–2). These twelve men were certainly not qualified to do these things. They brought no special character or gifts for any of these tasks; they were men whom most people would consider insignificant members of the larger society. The only distinction they could claim was that they had been watching and following Jesus.

Jesus did not train these men to conduct synagogue services or to maintain the routines of the synagogue. His mission was to the multitudes of harassed and helpless that he encountered in the villages and towns. Jesus focused all his energy on the mission of the Father, and he sent his disciples out on the same mission, two by two. He didn't go with them; he didn't control them; he didn't try to make sure they did it "right." In fact, he insisted that they go with as few resources as possible, "no staff, no bag, no bread, no money, no extra shirt" (Luke 9:3). We learn that they followed his instructions and imitated his practice, and their ministry gave them, and Jesus, much joy and satisfaction.

We might ask, was Jesus leading or managing his disciples? I suggest that Jesus was leading them, defining the vision of the kingdom of God that was before them, empowering them to make decisions on their own, and then motivating and inspiring them to follow his lead.

Reflecting on the case study of Gerald and Joshua, we realize that although Gerald himself was charged to manage the established ministries of his mission, he understood and embraced the pattern Jesus employed to make disciples. Mentoring out of a position of equality—he and Joshua were "fifty-fifty"—and even weakness, Gerald over time equipped Joshua so that he no longer needed Gerald to hold him up. By the time Gerald had completed his missionary term, he had released and empowered Joshua to carry on the preaching ministry of these congregations. However, Gerald's missionary successors liked preaching, took back the preaching role, and reduced Joshua and others to interpreters once again.

For Gerald, releasing these young men was an act of faith and trust. He understood the key principle that the work and the outcome of that work are God's and not the mentor's. Gerald released the responsibility of these congregations to others and entrusted them to carry on this ministry without his guiding presence.

We may conclude then that a mentor who has the goal of multiplying leaders must not focus on managing, unless the goal is to produce managers who can help a leader accomplish the leader's purpose. A mentor who wants to equip leaders must focus on equipping these leaders to do the work and then release control. Releasing control requires our sacrificing the right to ensure the intended outcome of a ministry. The mentor must take the risk of letting go and trusting that God will accomplish the purpose.

The Risk of Releasing Control

A brief review of mission history shows that most mission agencies and missionaries have a great deal of difficulty releasing control. As Tom Steffen has noted in his classic study *Passing the Baton: Church Planting That Empowers* (1997), most mission agencies do not have a plan to release control and leave. Steffen argues that this is a significant flaw in mission strategy and ultimately keeps the people whom they have mentored from carrying on the ministry and being a self-sustaining, self-supporting church.

Missionaries who give their lives to career mission service often understand their role to mean that they will be in control until they leave their ministry. This is tragically the wrong perspective on the empowering of God's people and the expansion of the work of the kingdom of God. Again Weaver's study (2004) in Hungary is a wonderful case in point. The Hungarian leaders who were effective in empowering others continually multiplied their ministries and released them to the people they had trained. Weaver notes that these pastors gave significant time and investment to the biblical training of these men and women and provided personal support to help them be effective in their ministries. They did not abandon them, but they released them to do the work, foregoing control in order to encourage the expansion of ministry and to achieve a vision focused on the mission of God in their city.

The most essential act in empowering others to achieve a compelling vision of faith is that of releasing control. For many of us, this is the most difficult act of will. When we release control, we entrust others to act in ways that may not fit with our idea of how they should act. We take the risk that whatever task or responsibility we have released will not be done in accord with our design, and in the worst case, we are willing to accept failure on the part of others with all its consequences. By releasing control, we are saying that we will relinquish our right to assure that the desired effects occur, and we do so in faith that God, working through people, will accomplish the divine purpose. That is, we decide to trust both the Holy Spirit and the people God has called and is using.

The risk of letting go is great. Some may judge us to be inept because we have not controlled outcomes that seem essential to process and progress. We ourselves will feel anxiety and stress because the things that we believe are important may not happen in the way that we desire. The disciplines we think are essential to success may not be followed. The outcomes may be disastrous for the group and for the individuals involved.

Releasing control then is a significant act of faith and trust, both in God and in the person(s) released. The leader who decides to relinquish power is placing trust in the empowered person and in God that the power given will be used to accomplish God's purpose. This is why power giving is an act of faith and grace; the outcome rests in the power and grace of God. Only by faith in the power of God and in the power of the living Word can we let go of our desire to control and place the responsibility for outcomes in the hands of others and of God. Jesus's act of releasing the leadership of the church to the Twelve is the penultimate illustration of this principle. In spite of their failures before and after his resurrection, Jesus trusted them and many others, empowered by the Holy Spirit, to do his work and establish his church.

10

Responsible-*To* Leadership

What Are Marta's Responsibilities? A Case Study

Marta was a European missionary working in Indonesia with her international mission organization (IMO) and a local mission affiliate (LMA). Her director assigned her to provide oversight for the literacy and leadership training staff of the local mission, to pay these local workers from IMO funds, and to keep the accounting records for her mission. Marta had three local literacy teachers on her team: Bizu, Ezra, and Nehemiah.

Marta was always frustrated with the way the local mission director supervised his local workers. As the accountant for the IMO, she saw that the local mission director kept no records and provided no accountability to the local workers. She often complained to her IMO director about the sloppiness of local leadership and responsibility. In the local mission culture, monthly support was not related to work; money involved having a position and income to supplement gardens and other jobs. The local mission did not expect its staff to work full time. Work reports were not required, but Marta's best teacher, Ezra, gave them over the radio regularly. Marta also sent the local director reports of plans and progress, something she started when she took this assignment. Before that nobody had asked or commented about the work or the productivity of the local team.

Bizu gave Marta the most difficulty. She noticed that when Bizu worked with her in the office, minor things just disappeared. After two years of work, he became critical, and the quality of his work deteriorated. One day he said that he was tired of correcting Marta's mistakes on the literacy lessons she printed for him. When she asked what was wrong, he said there was no problem. However, Bizu lied about his work; he drew his food and travel allowance for a week, but worked only one morning and then went to another island to sell his cash crop. While there, he was caught stealing money by the police. When the news reached the local church, they suspended him from his teaching position for one year.

When the suspension was over and the local mission director did not approach him to resume his work, Bizu announced in a district church meeting that if the mission did not rehire him the entire literacy program would stop. This threat was directed toward his national colleagues. At first the local area director did not want Bizu back, but because Bizu insisted on having regular monthly pay, he was granted a new position as adult literacy and Bible teacher. Marta, in her pain about this man and his lack of responsibility, took the opportunity in another church meeting to recite all of Bizu's failings to the whole congregation. To her surprise Bizu apologized in a roundabout way, saying he was sorry about the good and bad things he had done. When she asked other people to clarify what he meant, Nehemiah said that Bizu had not acknowledged any of his wrongs.

Marta was deeply frustrated and discouraged about this situation. She felt that she had no authority to do the work assigned her, and she was deeply discouraged about her relationship with the local mission. She did not feel that her director in the IMO supported her when she reported to him the mismanagement of the local leader and staff. Although Ezra and Nehemiah were good workers and a source of encouragement to her, she could not understand why the local director and the church did not fire Bizu. Further, she was deeply hurt when the LMA director told her that she had no authority regarding Bizu's accountability or work performance. After six years of work in this area, she felt responsible for all these problems; although she faithfully reported to her director and the local director, she could not understand why they failed to act on her reports.

Responsible-*For* or Responsible-*To*?

Many years ago I sat with my family in a group counseling session with a psychologist at Liebenzell Mission USA, where we were contributing to candidate orientation for ministry. As the psychologist explored with me and other members of my family our relationships of power with one another, he discerned quickly that my daughter and I were emotionally wrestling over power issues. After engaging both of us with some pointed questions, he turned to me. "Sherwood, do you feel responsible for your daughter?" I had to confess that, indeed, I did feel responsible for her. He then made this statement, which I have never forgotten: "Sherwood, you must be responsible *to* your daughter, but you cannot be responsible *for* her. She is responsible for her own actions."

The core issue here was my emotional attachment and my felt need to assure that my daughter did not do things that would be harmful to her or to the family. Responsible-*for* thinking and emotions led me to use power and control to assure my teenage daughter's security and appropriate behavior. This kind of thinking assumes that the other person is unready and inadequate to act responsibly without my intervention. It also assumes that I know best, and that if I keep control, the results that I seek will be secured.

Responsible-*to* thinking and emotions begin with emotional detachment. I no longer see myself as the agent responsible for the behaviors of my daughter, but rather I see my daughter as the agent, and I, her father, must act responsibly *to* her as a person who will determine her own thinking, actions, and outcomes. This kind of thinking assumes that the other person is responsible, adequate, and will decide what the best course of action will be to achieve the results desired. It also assumes that I, her father, still have a role to play, granting authority and providing counsel, freedom, and accountability.

I recall an incident from my teenage years that illustrates how my father used emotional detachment and responsible-*to* leadership in mentoring me. Working alongside my father, I learned as a young teen how to wash and wax automobiles. When I was about fifteen years old, our next-door neighbor invited me to wash and wax her car. I accepted with enthusiasm and worked more than five hours to complete the task. When I was finished, I went to my father and asked him to come and inspect the job. He asked, "Did you do a good job?" I replied, "Yes!" He then said, "Are you satisfied with how it looks?" Again I said, "Yes!" He then said, "That's all I need to know," and he refused to accompany me to look at the car. I was angry and disappointed. I wanted him to look and to tell me my work was good. Instead, he taught me that I was the best judge of the quality of my work, and that if I was satisfied with the results, he had nothing more to add. This action shifted the focus of our relationship, so that from this point on he mentored me from a responsible-*to*, rather than a responsible-*for*, relationship. Less than a year later, he invited me to preach my first sermon during our Wednesday evening prayer meeting, granting me the authority, providing counsel when I asked, and giving me freedom to prepare and speak as I felt led by the Holy Spirit. After I had presented that message, he affirmed the positive result of my preparation and delivery and invited me to further disciplined study and preaching, which has become a lifelong work of ministry.

Responsible-*For* and Responsible-*To* Leadership

Responsible-*for* leaders demonstrate emotional attachment to their role and results, and they exercise power and control to achieve results and assure quality. In contrast, responsible-*to* leaders demonstrate emotional detachment from their role and results, and they grant authority, responsibility, and freedom to other people, whom they then counsel and hold accountable to achieve results and quality. Responsible-*for* leadership cannot relinquish control, since the leader is emotionally attached to both his or her role and to the achievement of results. A responsible-*to* leader places responsibility for results on the members of the team (which ideally is committed to covenant community) and trusts God for the wisdom to provide the counsel and accountability essential for each member.

In the case study above, Marta has a clear sense of responsibility *for* the operations and the results of the ministry that she is doing in partnership with a local church and the indigenous mission organization (LMA). That sense of responsibility comes first from her default culture, learned as a child in her family in Europe, and then from the socialization and attachment to the roles assigned to her by the IMO, the LMA, and the members of her team. How she approaches that responsibility is part of her personality and what she has learned about how to play her roles. Her emotions at the time of the story are of deep frustration with her directors and her team and disappointment in herself and her team members. She feels that she is not managing effectively either the operations or the results of her team, and that her directors are not supporting her. Having lapsed into criticism and condemnation of her local colleague Bizu, she also feels that she has failed spiritually.

Marta does not have a leadership role. She is clearly a middle manager, assigned by her mission to manage a project and to provide financial and progress reports in partnership with the local mission and the ministry team selected by the local church. Many Christian workers find themselves in middle-management roles and experience similar frustrations. As managers they must define goals for the project, plan and budget project activities, organize the work to get it done, control spending, and focus on achieving the anticipated results. They have not been given responsibility for defining vision or for motivating and inspiring people to work to fulfill the vision. Like Marta, they often feel unsupported by their leaders, responsible for things they cannot control, and frustrated by the poor performance of others with whom they work.

Marta finds herself in the same emotional situation I experienced years ago in my relationship with my daughter. Marta feels responsible *for* the funds allocated to the project, *for* the implementation of a work plan that the IMO asked her to create, and *for* proper management of funding distributed through the local mission director and the local church. She has found that all these responsibilities are out of her control and has deep anxiety and discouragement about them.

Responsible-*For* Behaviors

To illustrate the dilemma of middle managers on this topic, I will examine in depth the issue of accountability for funds in the case study of Marta and her ministry partners. Marta disclosed to her IMO supervisor that she felt responsible *for* what local mission and church leaders did with project funds, and that she had little control over LMA expenses and team performance (table 10.1). Lacking other power, she complained to her IMO supervisor and to the local director about the fact that Bizu and other workers saw the money as pay for the position and not the work, and as a consequence, the work was not done. Angry that Bizu, after he had received project funds, did not do any evident work, she confronted the local director about Bizu's behavior. Her suspicions about Bizu were confirmed when he was caught stealing in the port town.

Table 10.1 Responsible-*For* and Responsible-*To* Behaviors

Marta's Job	Responsible-*For*	Responsible-*To*
1. goals	1. define goals	1. shared vision, goals
2. work plan	2. organize work	2. discern gifts, match work
3. supervision	3. manage employees	3. mentor teammates
4. budget	4. set budget	4. facilitate budget
5. expense report	5. control expenses	5. facilitate reporting
6. results report	6. assure results	6. affirm results
7. liaison IMO/ LMA	7. assure LMA quality	7. interpret LMA values
	8. meet IMO goals	8. interpret IMO goals
		9. report team results

She was also deeply frustrated by the local director. When she complained to him about Bizu, he rebuked her and told her that the local church, not Marta, was responsible for disciplining her coworkers. She noticed how her coworkers took project materials without asking, how they used project time for personal activities, and she reported these things to the local director. Again, he reminded her that project work was part-time and that these men had to provide for their families. This did not relieve Marta of her internal sense of failure.

Marta was very pleased with Ezra, who actively prepared the reports she had requested in the project plan. She reminded the local director that Ezra and Nehemiah were faithful in their work, and Bizu was not. At the same time, she obliquely complained that she and they never received feedback on their reports and did not know if the local mission was satisfied with the progress they had made in their literacy and Bible-teaching work.

Finally, Marta expressed her displeasure that the local director had invited Bizu to rejoin the team after his suspension by the church. In her eyes Bizu was irresponsible and used his relationships in the church to demand a job for which he did little work. She felt that *Bizu undermined her ability to manage the project and achieve the outcomes for which she felt responsible to the IMO.*

Responsible-*To* Behaviors

As we reflect on Marta's feelings and actions, we need to ask Marta the same question the psychologist asked me: "Marta, do you feel responsible *for* the team and the project?" As we reflect on the data, we realize that Marta could benefit from the same advice I received. "Marta, you must be responsible *to* your team and directors, but you cannot be responsible *for* them. They are responsible for their own actions." How would this change Marta's thinking and behavior? And would these changes have any impact on the operations and results of her project?

First, Marta must cope with her internal emotional attachment to her role and results and agree that the local mission leader and her team members are responsible *for* their own choices and actions. Marta is responsible *to* the local leader and *to* her team to tell them what IMO leaders expect and desire with regard to budgeting and expense reporting, and she must work with them to create a budget and a process for reporting that they can actually use (table 10.1). Marta is also responsible *to* her IMO leaders to explain to them what she thinks has actually happened. Given their conflicting cultural values about work and compensation, Marta is not responsible for deciding if they did right or wrong. God is the only one who can judge "right or wrong" as a matter of heart. She may believe that they (the local leaders) did not do what the IMO leaders wanted or expected. If this is the case, she should ask the local director or her team members if her interpretation is true, or if they see it differently. It is very important that Marta understand, inasmuch as they are willing to tell her, how the local director and project workers see and understand their actions.

Marta should employ the "ask, seek, and knock" strategy (Willard 1998) in her relationships with these men. "Here is how I understand what has happened. Please correct me, or help me explain to my IMO supervisors how these funds have been used, and why. I want to support you and will do so if you help me to understand this more clearly."

If for some reason Marta thinks that this explanation is not satisfactory, she may say: "I will report exactly what you have told me; but you should know that they expect . . . , and what you have done does not meet their expectations. You (local leaders) are responsible *for* the use of these funds. I will report what you have done and your explanation of that. The IMO leaders will decide if they are satisfied."

Responsible-*to* behavior assumes that others are responsible for their own actions. The leader or manager must then act with integrity and love toward others on a team. The first requirement is that one is faithful in one's actions and responsibilities. The second is that one is faithful to our brothers and sisters in Christ, as participants together in covenant community.

Transforming a Dysfunctional Team

Marta's situation is unfortunately all too common in cross-cultural ministries. As we reflect on this case study, we realize that nearly everything that could go wrong has. Perhaps the most critical aspect is the absence of a community of trust that shares a common vision and commitment to mission. As Marta describes the situation, the vision that led to the establishment of the team has either been forgotten or was never shared by her local director and village associates. The villagers see the work of the team as a salaried position, gained through the church, that gives them financial benefits. Bizu seems to have no commitment to a vision or the work of the team, and Ezra and Nehemiah do the work, but we see no evidence of mission and purpose.

As a middle manager, Marta can and should be a leader. She is one of the faces of the original vision to this local community, and if she does not do her part to share and carry that vision, it will be lost. We do not know the history of the vision for this team, so we can only conjecture about its loss and recovery. Surely someone in the local church was partner to the original vision that led to the founding of the team. Likewise, the IMO director and the local director have some knowledge of the vision. When vision is lost, teams and projects become dysfunctional management nightmares of the kind that Marta has experienced. Marta is responsible *to* share the vision that brought her to this place. She is responsible *to* engage her team members around this vision and invite them into relationships of prayer and discussion that renew the vision for the whole team.

The second area of grave dysfunction on this team is the absence of attention to covenant community. Marta does not trust her directors and the members of her team. Likewise, they do not trust Marta. Although Marta does not have a position of leadership authority that empowers her to convene and engage people in building trust, she does have the responsibility *to* build trust with her coworkers. However, Marta has defaulted to responsible-*for* behaviors, focusing her energies on constructing project plans, defining work schedules, protecting the project materials, and producing project reports. Ezra has pleased her, because he has produced the kind of work that helps Marta feel successful as project manager. Nehemiah failed to please Marta in the early months of his work, but she now defines him as a "good worker." Marta has missed the Lord's priority for "loving our neighbors" and for "making disciples," an opportunity open to her in her relationships with Ezra, Nehemiah, and even perhaps with Bizu. Bizu's negative response to Marta has focused primarily on her concern about things and schedule, which grate against his default culture and personality.

Marta is handicapped in her role as a middle manager, feeling responsible *for* the good and the bad of the team, yet without authority and empowerment to lead or manage. In this her directors from both the IMO and the local mission have also failed as cross-cultural leaders. Neither has supported Marta in the work of sustaining vision and missional focus in the work of these local teams. Neither has encouraged or supported her in the work of creating a community of trust within their organizations. The agenda of each mission agency seems to lack focus on the essential elements of the mission of God and covenant community. Marta does not have the authority to *inspire and empower her team to achieve a compelling vision of faith.* As a manager caught between two organizations, she has only her influence as a committed follower of Jesus Christ to move people in this way. Her organizational leaders have failed her in a very significant way.

But Marta also has responsibility here. She is responsible *to* her directors to tell them that the vision has been lost in the local community, and that she needs their leadership to renew the vision and mobilize the local church and local mission staff to build the trust essential to be a missional community. Marta can play a key spiritual role in this very difficult and challenging situation; she can pray diligently for her leaders, asking God to renew their vision, and she can invite her team members to pray with her about the issues of vision and community. She can also quietly work with those in her sphere of relationships to share the vision God gave her to come to this place, and to invest her time, resources, and energy to build trust among her team members, their families, and the local church community. If Marta and these mission leaders would commit to building covenant community teamwork, they together would see profoundly improved results from this ministry.

Resisting the Urge to Give "Expert" Help

Because we are by nature power seekers, it is almost impossible for us to resist giving good advice to people whom we have empowered for ministry, especially when we believe it will make the work more effective and improve results. I frequently fall into this trap, and so did Marta. She saw her team and the local director making mistakes, she felt responsible for them, and she intervened by correcting their mistakes and offering unsolicited advice and direction, which she knew would make things work better. As we might expect, her local director and team members felt that Marta's advice was condemnation. When we intervene in this way, more often than not we alienate the very person we are trying to help. We push our good things on those we think need them, in hope of producing our intended effect in the world, using our power to bring about the things that will give *us* significance. Power-giving leadership resists the urge to do what Dallas Willard calls "condemnation engineering" (1998, 228).

How can we, the educated, the experienced, avoid this unfortunate liability of imposing our expertise to improve the work of others? First, we must learn the importance of waiting until we are asked, or, seeing a teammate in difficulty, we ask permission to offer help. Second, in giving advice we must learn to suggest options—two or three ways of solving a problem—so that those we wish to help can choose a solution rather than rely on our "correct" answer. And when we are asked, we must resist the temptation of doing the work for them or of showing them how by our expert performance. Our expert performance will only discourage the weak and dismay the novice. Our virtuosity must inspire but never demoralize. Thus if you are a great teacher, you should teach only in contexts where you are not displacing some lesser teacher. If I am a great organizer, I should limit my organizing to those circumstances where it is my responsibility alone to organize; and I should empower others in their sphere of responsibility. Is this absurd? Should we not use our gifts for the kingdom of God? Of course. But our primary role should be to encourage, not to dominate. Encouragement is a spiritual gift. Domination is not.

The key lies in building relationships that lead to trust, influence, and encouragement for the work and purpose of God. If our desire is to truly foster followers of Christ, then we must submit our concern for results to the Lord and surrender our powers of teaching, organizing, and leading to those we are mentoring. When we place Jesus, rather than the quest for power and results, at the center of our being, we will look to the Spirit and Word of God to guide us. By setting an example as followers of Christ, we encourage those we mentor to develop their obedience to the Spirit and grow in skills of service as they also follow the Lord Jesus Christ.

Responsible-*To*: Leading in Covenant Community

Leadership is always about results. The question is, who is responsible for the results? If we commence with the assumption that ministry teams must begin with God's priorities, that assumption changes how we answer the question. In chapter 5 I argued that God's highest priority is that we be and live as the people of God. The second priority is "striving together with one accord for the faith of the gospel" of Jesus Christ (Phil. 1:27). God then is the one who is responsible for results, and we are responsible to "strive together with one accord" as members of the body of Christ. It is my argument here that responsible-*to* leadership enables the body to serve and God to work in that body to accomplish God's results.

In his letter to Philippian believers, the apostle Paul highlights several principles that I deem essential for responsible-*to* leadership. First, God does the work, "being confident of this, that he who began a good work in you will carry it on to completion until the day of Christ Jesus" (Phil. 1:6). Second, the responsibility rests on the members of the body, "whether I come and see you or only hear about you in my absence, I will know that you stand firm in the one Spirit, striving together" (Phil. 1:27). Third, the body must work together, "being one in spirit and of one mind. . . . In humility value others above yourselves, not looking to your own interests but each of you to the interests of the others" (Phil. 2:2–4).

In this context Timothy is Paul's middle manager, delegated to visit these people, get a report of their ministry, and encourage them. Paul affirms Timothy's authority, responsibility, and readiness to serve: "I have no one else like him, who will show genuine concern for your welfare. For everyone looks out for their own interests, not those of Jesus Christ. But you know that Timothy has proved himself, because as a son with his father he has served with me in the work of the gospel" (Phil. 2:20–22). If I may reflect on the story about my father and me and waxing the car, my father concluded that I had proved myself, and he no longer needed to check my work and refused to do so. Here Paul is affirming an even greater trust in Timothy and his utmost confidence in Timothy's leadership and service, forged in their partnership as father and son together for the gospel.

Finally, Paul speaks the truth in love and calls upon a local leader and the community to help together to resolve an internal conflict. "I plead with Euodia and I plead with Syntyche to be of the same mind in the Lord. Yes, and I ask you, my true companion, help these women since they have contended at my side in the cause of the gospel, along with Clement and the rest of my co-workers" (Phil. 4:2–3). Paul's plea here is for responsible-*to* intervention in a situation of conflict. We are given no other details, except that Paul encourages them to stand firm in the Lord and then gives thanks for their generosity and sharing in Paul's time of trouble.

When we act as if we are responsible *for*, we take power into our hands, and we use it to try to accomplish our outcomes, the results that we desire, in effect becoming power seekers. By being responsible *to*, however, we focus on the covenant community and empowering all the members of the body of Christ to produce the results that God intends for his church. The act of being responsible *to* involves asking appropriate questions, investing time in the building of relationships, and speaking truth in love at times when God directs us to do so. All members of the body have gifts and roles for service, and leaders encourage all to act responsibly and in obedience to Christ. The results belong to the Lord.

11

Exercising Power, Asking for Correction

Exercising Power in Thailand: A Case Study

Sam, an official from a Swiss foundation, came to Thailand to investigate and fund projects to assist economically disadvantaged people. Learning of a multicultural team working with urban homeless people, he contacted Sarah, one of the team members, and invited her to submit a proposal. In consultation with Marcus, the team leader, Sarah submitted a proposal for $55,000 to build six small houses that homeless people could use for temporary accommodation. During an interview, Sarah described the conflict that arose between the team and the team leader over these houses:

> We were all so thrilled when the application was successful, and the foundation transferred the full amount of $55,000 into our team account. We found a good team of builders, who built six lovely houses. The whole team got involved in painting and wallpapering, and the houses looked great! But then Marcus, our team leader and chief fundraiser, returned from an overseas trip. He said the houses were way too luxurious for temporary housing for the poor. He didn't like the wallpaper we had put up and gave orders to roughly paint over it. After agreeing that trees could be planted around the houses at a cost of $1,000, Marcus then changed his mind and insisted the trees be

removed. The whole team was so frustrated and upset that resources were being wasted. Personally, I was really embarrassed. I've been avoiding writing to Sam, because it's my credibility and integrity that's questioned if we misuse the funds donated by his foundation.

Marcus had formed this homeless ministry by gathering several wealthy Thai Christian believers together and sharing a vision to assist economically deprived people in Thailand. He had a particular concern for women and children, who, because of financial pressure, often drifted into prostitution. Motivated by Marcus's passion to make a difference in the lives of these people, the Thai Christians promised to help him financially when he put together a team to do the work. Building on their commitment, Marcus gathered several Thais, Sarah, and another Asian expatriate to organize and carry out diverse ministry projects.

From the beginning Marcus led this team by employing a Thai patron-client power model in which the leader often makes unilateral decisions and even reverses the decisions of those with less power. The team had the same vision but very different values underlying their decisions. As reported by Sarah, Marcus delegated decision making to them but then countermanded their decisions and forced them to destroy some of their work. Sarah and her Singaporean colleague expressed deep frustration, and the Thai team members, who accepted the patron-client model of leadership, felt a loss of face in the way Marcus countermanded their work. During Lorraine Dierck's visits to this team, several team members expressed frustration, stating that the team had become totally ineffective in meeting their ministry goals (adapted with permission from Dierck 2007, 167–69).

Exercising Power to Achieve Results

One may have presumed from the earlier chapters that leading should not employ the exercise of power. Nothing could be further from the truth. As I stated in chapter 9, power exchanges pervade nearly all relationships, and the exercise of power is an essential part of leading and following. Leaders and followers have power, and they must learn how to use their power constructively in covenant community and to accomplish kingdom work. Marcus failed this test on two measures:

he did not exercise his power constructively, and he did not invest in building covenant relationships, perhaps lacking understanding of how to lead in covenant community. As a consequence he impaired his team, and the results of their work fell far short of their potential. A leader must use power in such a way that the team is motivated to higher levels of achievement.

Richard Wood suggests that one of the most important functions of a leader is to keep the team or organization focused on its mission (2006, 218). In the case study above, we see that Marcus has been partially effective on that count. Thais and expatriates alike are deeply committed to their ministry to the urban homeless. But vision alone cannot create unity of purpose, and conflict about decisions and their implementation has created a crisis that at best has demoralized the team and compromised its mission. Marcus has acted arbitrarily, over-ruled decisions made by team members, and forced them to destroy work they had completed. He has wasted the time and resources of his team in what seemed to them to be capricious acts of power.

Although Marcus might argue that he is acting in an appropriate Thai "patron" role, he has misunderstood the Thai hierarchical exercise of power. Marcus has not learned either the important Thai value for con-sulting with one another nor what Richard Mouw calls "*shared* leader-ship" founded on New Testament teaching about our sinfulness and the diversity of gifts given to us in the body of Christ (2006, 129). Lorraine Dierck (2007) reports that Thais place very high value on consultation together before a decision is made; after that consultation has taken place, Thais recognize and accept the right of a leader to make the decision. But it should be done in such a way that the people involved do not lose face. Marcus violated both of these cultural principles, failing to consult and causing his whole team to feel compromised and lose face.

Marcus has also failed to exercise what Mouw, taking his cue from James MacGregor Burns, calls "transforming leadership [in which] both leader and follower are raised to higher levels of motivation and morality, so that each is changed in the process" (2006, 126). Mouw goes on to explain that, while positional authority is legitimate in Christian community, it must be tempered to assure that all members of the body are able to exercise their gifts effectively (2006, 129). This means that a leader must delegate authority to others with different gifts and then release control, entrusting others to use authority and power appropriate to their roles in the community and the body of Christ.

What if this team had been organized around a different social game, such as the egalitarian game? Would that have solved the problem of the abuse of leadership authority and the exercise of power? The group, or strong members of a group, has all the potential to misuse power that we see in this patron-client team (Koeshall 2008, 265–66). Further, Wood notes that "servant" (power-giving) leadership cannot be effective without an appropriate use of the "powers of office," even and especially in organizations that seek to operate on the basis of consensus (2006, 216). Wood observes that teams accustomed to making decisions by consensus are often held hostage by one strong member, who blocks the group and may actually dictate the decision by the act of resisting consensus.

In his discussion of how egalitarian Quaker meetings are "biased toward inaction," Wood suggests that one of the most important powers of a leader is to "require dialog." He goes on to say, "To use power to require dialog or suspend the status quo is to lead from vulnerability, for it involves taking the risk in opening an issue without controlling the outcome. But it also frees the assigned leader to be a participant in seeking a new solution" (2006, 219–20). I concur with his observation and would extend its application to all the social games of work and leadership.

The exercise of power for the common good of the covenant community is a responsibility of those assigned leadership roles. Anita Koeshall (2008, 268) argues that leaders and followers live in community together as "redeemed agents," and as such they each are responsible both to lead and to follow. When leaders exercise "redeemed power," they engage in "self-emptying for the sake of others" (2008, 260), rather than acting to increase their authority, control, and "power distance" (Hofstede 2001). When "redeemed agents" lead and follow in covenant community, they create a "dynamic asymmetry . . . that critiques both oppressive hierarchy and competitive, controlling egalitarianism" (2008, 268).

Leading for results is at its best when leaders and groups understand how and when to use power and when to give it away. Mouw clarifies how an effective leader delegates responsibility and power to others in the body, thus sharing leadership and strengthening the team or organization by increasing its capacity to serve with the full range of spiritual and natural gifts. Wood helps us understand the critical importance and power of dialogue to build effective communication and empower others to exercise their creative gifts to advance the mission. When a leader focuses on the common good, delegates responsibility and power to others, and employs the power of dialogue and effective communications, that leader motivates and enables a team to achieve its maximum potential and results.

Asking for Correction

Over the course of our consulting ministry with mission organizations in Africa and Asia, my wife and I have found that missionary and national leaders are frequently involved in conflict with each other. As we explore more deeply the causes of those conflicts, we find that each group of leaders has proceeded to decisions and action based on their own understanding of the situation without significant dialogue with others. Like Marcus, who reached decisions in isolation from his team members about the housing project, many project leaders we have observed present a decision as an accepted fact to their colleagues. Although they may not have the power to order the others to do what they have decided, they have failed in precisely the same way that Marcus has failed.

One of the most common flaws of leaders is their failure to ask for correction, and when they receive it, to accept it and learn from it. In his discussion of Jewish doctrines of leadership, Elliot Dorff declares that people must learn "to evaluate their leaders' performance so that they can be justly criticized, corrected, and in the extreme, rejected as a leader. . . . To be a mature leader or follower requires a keen sense of *judgment*; without that the followers become infants, the leaders become gods, and following them becomes an exercise in idolatry" (2006, 17–18). According to Dorff's insights, effective leaders encourage and empower followers to evaluate effectively their performance. This must be built into our understanding of covenant community and social game. Regardless of, and appropriate to, the social game employed, a team must plan and implement processes that check and correct its leaders.

The work of designing process and empowering followers and leaders to participate in feedback is a complex agenda. In a situation where a single person, such as Marcus, is organizing a team, that person must act intentionally to create an open door for correction while in the process of forming covenant community. In a situation where two groups are seeking to partner, or two or three expatriates are seeking to bring two or three language communities together around common interests, the question of feedback and correction must be faced at the very beginning of negotiating relationships. If the leaders are going to give covenant community priority in these relationships, the feedback process is the obvious place to begin.

Pathways to Correction

While teaching and learning the core biblical values of community, leaders and followers must ask how to speak "truth in love" to one another. What is an acceptable process—confronting face-to-face, one person to another, or storytelling about a third-person outsider, or sending a mediator, or a periodic team meeting to ask, "how are we doing?" or a periodic survey, or "time out" for crisis dialogue? Identifying one or more acceptable processes will be contingent on the default cultures of the people involved and the social games they are most comfortable playing. Whatever the process or processes adopted by a team or partners, the followers must learn how to appropriately use them and be invited and encouraged by the leaders to do so.

Followers must have means to challenge leaders that are consistent with biblical commands to love one another and at the same time to question without condemning. Reflecting on the case study of Marcus and Sarah, we see that Sarah disagreed strongly with his decision to paint over the wallpaper and remove the trees. She also was embarrassed by his decisions on behalf of the team and afraid of what Sam might think about how they had misused funds. We know that the team operated as a corporate group with a strong patron-client bent. Marcus felt free to override team decisions. If Marcus had anticipated such conflict and wanted his team to be a covenant community, how would he have prepared Sarah and others to respond to such a situation?

Table 11.1 offers alternative ways of addressing these issues, depending on the emotions and reasoning of followers. Marcus, as leader, is responsible for training his team to confront him in ways that will motivate him to listen and help him to make wise decisions and correct his errors. He and the team are more inclined to respect and love one another if they learn how to confront in love. If Marcus had encouraged Sarah to let him know when she was hurt or embarrassed, she would have had more courage to speak to him about his decision to paint the wallpaper. If he had given his team permission to say, "We don't agree with this decision," they may have had the courage to tell him that his decision to remove the trees was unwise and could actually hinder future funding from the Swiss foundation.

Table 11.1 Challenging Leaders through Covenant Relationships

Covenant Community Emotions	1. We are hurting (for others).
	2. We are disappointed.
	3. We are embarrassed or ashamed.
	4. We are angry.
Covenant Community Thinking	1. What is not working?
	2. Help us understand.
	3. We disagree.
	4. Could we discuss other alternatives?

The social-game values of team members limit the options for confrontation open to them (see table 11.2). If they are Thais, they will be very reluctant to challenge someone who is of higher status and in a leadership position. To confront a leader is impossible for them, unless the leader invites them to participate in a discussion about a decision before it is made. Once the leader has made a bad decision, they will passively accept it and grieve quietly about the loss of face. In a weak corporate environment such as the one Marcus created, the only way he might discern people's anguish is by observing their silence and withdrawal. This is a sure sign that something is wrong, and he should ask them gently to tell him what has gone wrong. He could also ask Sarah, who may serve as a mediator for them, and with her Western values is more able to tell him openly why they are silent.

Sarah and her other Asian colleague may feel more free to report to him the feelings of the team, if he is willing to ask. If Marcus had prepared them during their training to share their concerns and emotions about his leadership, they would have been more likely to tell him either face-to-face or in a note or e-mail that team members were grieving about his decision to paint over the wallpaper. Sarah comes from a cultural background that permits confrontation but seldom uses it. Her Singaporean colleague also comes from an Asian culture that is more accepting of confrontation.

The case study suggests that Marcus had failed to empower his team members to confront him in any way. He expected them to do what he told them, and he did not welcome any negative feedback. As a consequence, he treated the team as servants, not understanding God's call for him to be accountable to the body of Christ in which he served. He failed to be either a servant or a transforming leader; he instead used his power to control and achieve the lesser goods of satisfying his own values and objectives and somehow to feel good about ministering to the poor, but not to the body of which he was an integral part.

Table 11.2 Social-Game Strategies for Challenging Leaders

Individualist (Weak Group)	1. Face-to-face confrontation 2. Group-to-group confrontation 3. Public argument 4. Public negotiation
Collectivist (Strong Group)	1. Observation of withdrawal behavior 2. Indirect storytelling 3. Letters or e-mail 4. Group discussions
Corporate (Strong Group)	1. Letters or e-mail 2. Mediation 3. Focus-group discussions 4. Compensation
Bureaucratic (Strong Group)	1. Informal, private confrontation (letter, report to supervisor) 2. Formal, open confrontation 3. Focus-group listening 4. Survey

Correction as Power Giving

The ultimate act of power giving, even more important than acceptance, is inviting others to critique one's work and decision making. Because missionaries and mission organizations, who control key resources, hold a structural power relationship with national churches, they may and often do make decisions that have a negative impact on the church without inviting any feedback. When we engage others in such a way as to solicit their reflection, feedback, and interpretation of our decisions, we create an environment of humility, empowering them to help us be more effective in our ministry.

Power-giving leadership invites others to critique one's work and decisions. By patiently listening and intentionally hearing what others say, we may correct our own structural rigidity and thereby become better able to work together for the purposes of the kingdom of God. The goal is to engage others in such a way that we empathize with their critique, build mutual understanding, and commit to a community relationship with them. By inviting them to critique our decisions and work, we open the door for greater understanding. By being willing to adjust and change what we do to better minister to them, we in fact create deeper community in Christ and greater capacity to love one another.

Part 4

Leading Cross-Culturally

12

The Challenge of Cross-Cultural Leadership

As we reflect on the case studies presented in this book, we see leaders struggling to be effective in their particular ministry settings. Some of them failed utterly in leading their multicultural teams. Others were only partially successful. All of them in some way or another failed to achieve their personal goals for leadership and ministry and the ideals that we set forth in the definition of leading cross-culturally at the beginning of this book. In the pages that follow, I will again reflect briefly on the question, why is leading so difficult?

Once again, *leading cross-culturally is inspiring people who come from two or more cultural traditions to participate with you in building a community of trust, and then to follow you and be empowered by you to achieve a compelling vision of faith.* What then are those challenges that keep us from fulfilling our vision and aspirations as God's servants, to lead cross-cultural or multicultural teams, extending God's healing reign in our broken world?

Playing with the Team God Gives You

Leadership on any team is only as good as the people whom God provides for that team. Returning once again to the analogy of sports, I noted in chapter 1 that in the summer of 2007 the Philadelphia Phillies professional baseball team achieved a landmark of ten thousand losses over their one-hundred-year history, more than any other professional sports team. Part of the challenge of leading the Phillies has been the need for each leader to play the game with the players that the owners hired. As we consider their record of ten thousand losses, it is clear that the Philadelphia Phillies teams for that one-hundred-year period consisted of people who were not the best baseball players in America. For some who accept leadership, a weak team becomes a very difficult challenge. I remember during my early years as provost and senior vice president of Biola University, I complained to God about some of the people on my team. I asked God, why this person, and why not someone who is more effective? I remember praying, "Please remove this person from leadership and give me someone else who can do the job more effectively." God's answer to this prayer was, "Absolutely no; don't you understand my work?" I learned over a period of time that God loves weak people and that God intends leaders to work with the people whom God gives to them. I was challenged when I read the prayer of our Lord Jesus Christ in John 17:

> I pray for them. I am not praying for the world, but for those you have given me, for they are yours. All I have is yours, and all you have is mine. And glory has come to me through them. . . . While I was with them, I protected them and kept them safe by that name you gave me. None has been lost except the one doomed to destruction so that Scripture would be fulfilled. . . . My prayer is not that you would take them out of the world but that you protect them from the evil one. (vv. 9–10, 12, 15)

Through reflection on Jesus's prayer, I at last understood that Jesus valued every one of the disciples whom the Father had given to him and was rejoicing that none of them had been lost. Examining what the Scriptures said about each disciple, I discovered that they were indeed a motley group of characters with many different flaws and weaknesses. Peter had denied him, Thomas doubted him, Philip questioned him, and each of them in his own way challenged Jesus regarding who Jesus was and what he was doing. It suddenly dawned on me that the people whom God had given me were my gift and my glory. My responsibility was similar to that of the Jesus whom I sought to follow—to keep them, treasure them, help them to become all that God intended for them, and pray for them to be effective in the world and not removed from it. I repented of my prayer asking God to remove people from my leadership team.

At the same time, leaders have the challenge of weak people and occasionally bad people. In the case studies recounted in this book, weak people have certainly been part of all the different multicultural teams, and a few teams have had one or two who may have been a destructive presence. Such is the nature of teamwork and leadership. As we seek to follow Christ, we must search the Scriptures to discern how Jesus and the apostles dealt with bad people and with weak people and must follow Jesus in this process.

As we reflect on the case studies in this book, we see that each leader struggled with emotional and irrational responses by people on their team. Again, this is part of the work of leadership. I remind students in my classes that we are first emotional creatures and only secondarily rational. As we respond to crises or stressful situations in leadership, we rarely operate based on reason and rational processes. When things get tough, we first respond emotionally—frustration, anger, fear, disappointment, and betrayal. These emotions often get the best of us, leading us to seek power to protect ourselves, which in turn undermines the will and purpose of God. Knowing our emotional makeup, the evil one attacks us through our undisciplined emotional life. Working on teams, we must understand that our responsibility in the body is to practice spiritual disciplines and community fellowship that enable us to mediate our emotional responses in Christ.

Westerners, educated to trust the power of reason and rationality, assume that people will act responsibly and rationally. This is a false assumption. Most of us, if we are honest in our self-assessment, will recognize that we often act first from our emotional being. The natural consequence of this attribute of human experience and response is that leading a multicultural team always involves irrational and emotional relationships.

The practice of judging and condemning is another canker afflicting teamwork. As a leader, I must acknowledge that this problem is "my problem," and it is also the problem of the people with whom I work. We make assumptions about others' motives, and if we do not agree with what they are doing or if their motives seem suspect, we fall into the sin of judgment and condemnation. Even though we know that Jesus has absolutely forbidden this practice (Matt. 7:1–12), we resort to it regularly in our leadership and teamwork. This practice of judgment and condemnation is one of the most destructive practices of human life. People in cultures around the world use it on a daily basis to control the behavior of members of their communities. A quick review of the case studies in this volume will show that judgment and condemnation are at least a small part of every case. This is an endemic part of pastoral failure, mission leadership failure, and team leadership failure. It is also a pervasive problem in teams trying to work cross-culturally.

Again, Marguerite Shuster points to the way of Christ (1987, 237–43). We are called not to the way of power and condemnation but to the way of prayer and praise. We are only capable of working effectively when we are willing to confess our sins to one another and pray together in team relationships, allowing the power of God to transform us from judgment and condemnation to forgiveness, acceptance, and unity. The Scriptures repeatedly remind us that we are to pray for peace, we are to overcome evil with good, and we are to forgive even as the Lord has forgiven us. The only way that we can achieve this kind of teamwork is through a commitment to confessing our sins to one another and to praying for and with one another. Only after prayer, acceptance, and praise to God may the peace of Christ rule in our hearts and in our teamwork.

What If They Don't Fit?

The question of fit is complex, involving every aspect of human life—personality, spiritual gifting, social values, worldview, relational congeniality, maturity, family obligations, motivation, ambition, and so on. As we reflect on the case studies in this volume, we see a variety of these factors at work. Pastor David (chapter 8) made a decision almost as soon as he was appointed to dismiss the three associate pastors on his staff. We can only conjecture as to why, but perhaps he feared they would be loyal to the former pastor, or that they were rivals for his position, or that they did not fit his vision for the ministry of the church. The story makes it clear that this decision created team conflict over a period of three years until each of these men found other ministry opportunities. Pastor David did not consider these men to be God's gift to him, and in that I believe he erred.

How do we know God's will in these situations? The Scriptures provide counsel and guidelines for us, if we are willing to listen and put them into practice. For example, in the case of Pastor David, I would counsel him to begin with a season (two or three months) of prayer for and observation of these three men. What is God doing through them in the congregation? How are they responding to support the elders and David in their ministries? What are their spiritual and ministry gifts, and how is the Holy Spirit working through them in the congregation? During this time Pastor David, as leader, must proactively demonstrate his love and acceptance of these men in their ministries. If they sense they are on trial or not accepted, that will provoke anxiety and resistance.

After watching and listening to the Holy Spirit, Pastor David may take the initiative to sit down with each man and begin a conversation about his calling, giftedness, and aspiration for ministry. By this time David has observed the strengths and weaknesses of each and the investments they have made in ministries, and he has a better understanding of how each might contribute to the vision that God has given him. I would counsel Pastor David to assume that God has each of these men serving in this local church for a purpose, and that David is part of God's ongoing work in their lives. David then must prayerfully ask, "How, Lord, may I serve your purpose in the life and work of each of these men?" The issue is not "my team" but rather the "body of Jesus Christ" and my role to minister to that body.

Pastor David may in fact find that God is calling one or all of these men to serve in other ministries, and that he is able to mentor and encourage each one to take the next step at the right time and for the right purpose. But he may also find that God brought one or more of these men to this church to support him and enhance his ministry. He cannot discern this unless he is willing to watch and pray, and to prayerfully engage each person on issues of calling, giftedness, and commitment to this team and ministry. I have found in my own leadership that when I take the time and effort to prayerfully help people understand their gifts and calling, our decision to not renew a contract, while still painful, becomes an opportunity to explore further God's will and purpose in their lives.

What If They Drag the Team Down?

Marta, the middle manager serving to facilitate a local literacy and translation team (chapter 10), had a deep relational and emotional conflict with Bizu, one of three national team members. Bizu did many things to frustrate Marta, so many that she despaired for the ministry and her ability to continue serving the team. She struggled with Bizu's work habits and values about work, money, materials, and productivity. She was uncomfortable just being around him, and his habits and behaviors often seemed unethical by her standards of morality. Bizu had family and financial pressures that Marta did not understand, and he used church and community relationships to coerce her and the team into concessions that she believed were detrimental to their ministry. Marta wanted to get rid of Bizu, and she prayed that the LMA or the local church would refuse to allow him to return to the team after his time of discipline had ended. Was God's will thwarted when the local director and the church restored Bizu to his position?

Marta's struggle with Bizu is more complex than Pastor David's situation with his three associates. Bizu is a member of the body of Christ, yet from Marta's perspective he is a carnal believer, whose selfish actions are destructive to her, the team, the project, and the church. What alternatives do we have when a person seems so destructive to the work of a team?

The principles of covenant community relationships must be the foundation of our leadership practices. I have been in situations very similar to Marta's and have found them painful and often impossible to resolve. When I have yielded to the temptation to use my power as a leader to impose a solution, the consequences have proven as painful as or worse than the troublesome situation. So my first counsel to Marta is to begin with prayer and reflection on Scripture and to keep praying until she has peace from the Lord about a plan of action to follow.

In a confrontation with the "Bizu" on my ministry team, I was prompted by the Holy Spirit to begin with the question, "I have observed your pain and frustration to the point of anger over the last several weeks. Why are you so angry with me and others on the team?" And then I listened. Soon it became apparent to me that my Bizu had been hurt many times by others on the team, over a period of several years. These hurts, without any resolution, had accumulated to the point that my Bizu felt angry most of the time. In my role as leader, I understood that my first task was to acknowledge that I and others on the team had wronged this Bizu, and I further promised to correct as many of these wrongs as possible at that time. Then I asked for forgiveness, which my Bizu granted.

One of my colleagues, Janice Strength, notes that saying "I was wrong" is far more powerful than saying "I am sorry." She notes that we often push children to say "I am sorry" when they and we know they are not. To acknowledge "I was wrong" is to take responsibility for the action we have done. In the confrontation with my Bizu, my acknowledgment of our wrongs and my assurance of action to correct many of them created an openness in this relationship that had not been present previously. At that point, I felt free in the Holy Spirit to move to confrontation (Gal. 6:1–3) about the pain this Bizu was causing in the team. I then spoke about my Bizu's pattern of judging and condemning other members of the team; I acknowledged that this was sometimes with good cause, but that in the body of Christ, it was not the way we should confront one another. In gentleness, I stated that I could no longer allow this pattern to continue, and if my Bizu refused to stop this condemning behavior, I would take further disciplinary action, such as suspension or dismissal from the team.

Pain—Schoolmaster for Change

The sad fact of human life is that people rarely change until they have experienced pain severe enough to force them to consider alternatives.

The apostle Paul faced as much internal conflict in his newly planted churches as we ever experience on ministry teams. The churches at Corinth and Philippi were wracked by internal dissent and bickering. His letters to these churches plead with these believers to focus on their mission, proclaiming the gospel of Jesus Christ, and to be of one mind (Phil. 2:1–5), considering others better than themselves. Yet, the evidence is that they too resisted change and persisted in living by the demands of the "flesh" rather than the gift of the Spirit.

People such as Bizu often have problems in their families, work, and other relationships; in their weakness they stumble, fall, and sometimes resort to destructive, sinful behaviors that damage them and the body of Christ. As leaders we have the responsibility to love them—acknowledging our own wrongs—to confront them, and to invite them to repentance and forgiveness. If they refuse to respond as a member of the body, then separation may be the appropriate next step.

We have seen in the case studies throughout this book that leaders and followers alike create significant pain for one another. If we are willing to consider that pain a warning and turn to the Scriptures for correction in our leadership and relationships, the Scriptures assure us that those who "walk by the Spirit" will inherit the kingdom of God (Gal. 5:13–25). For leaders and multicultural teams, this is a promise that in the midst of our pain and difficulties, we will indeed accomplish the mission of God.

13

The Hope of
Cross-Cultural Leadership

Several years ago Paul Locatelli, president of Santa Clara University, speaking to a large assembly of academic leaders in California, challenged these leaders with a statement that I will paraphrase as follows: "The primary question is not, are your values eroding? Values are always eroding. The primary question is, what are you doing to renew your values?" As I reflected on Locatelli's words and my leadership at Biola University, I recognized that the core values at Biola were routinely eroding, and as a leader I had not focused actively on how to renew those values. The same thing is true of the work of multicultural teams in mission. The task and the routines of daily work always erode our mission and vision for the ministry. They also erode our spiritual values. The question is not whether our values are eroding; team values are always eroding. The question is, what are we doing as leaders to renew our sense of mission, to restore our vision, and to renew the values that are critical for multicultural teamwork? Our hope for effective leadership and ministries lies in aligning ourselves with the mission and work of God in a lost and broken world.

Renewing Mission, Vision, and Values

As we reflect on the case studies and discussions in this volume, we conclude that one of the first things lost in multicultural teamwork is a focus on mission and vision. The case of the church planters, Galen, Kate, Henry, and Myra (chapter 1), documents how this wonderfully gifted team pressed so hard to achieve their goal of planting a viable church that they failed to accomplish their vision of equipping local leaders to plant churches. The viable church and the laudable creation of an Internet café business to provide work and evangelistic contacts for new Christians became ends in themselves. After eight years of work, this team despaired that their vision was lost.

In the pressures that we all experience from our respective constituencies, we become preoccupied with goals and accountability. Team leaders are often frustrated by the team's failure to reach goals in the time frame expected or to use funding or to be accountable in ways deemed appropriate by the constituency. As we saw clearly in the struggle between Sarah and Marcus in their ministry to the homeless in Thailand (chapter 11), frustration provokes us to focus inwardly and vent our emotions on one another. When we give in to the pressures of time, constituency, funding, and accountability, and they replace our sense of mission and purpose, we lose perspective on why we are working together and the vision that God has for this ministry as a team.

Every leader who expects and hopes to be effective in leading cross-culturally must give repeated attention to the mission, the vision, and the values that are essential to kingdom work. Every team meeting should include some intentional renewal of mission, vision, and/or values. As soon as that component of the team is lost, the mission and the vision will be lost to the routines and the pressures of doing our daily work. Every case study that we have considered here has suffered because of a loss of mission, vision, and/or values among the people who were part of the multicultural team process.

The Work of Renewal

The work of renewal must be intentional and become part of the routine agenda of a team or ministry group. After hearing Paul Locatelli's address, I returned to Biola and asked others, and myself, when did we last give attention to our mission and core values? Although we had spent considerable time reflecting on our mission in the community, I realized that a core value of our undergraduate program was a required year of biblical studies. During the eight years of my leadership as chief academic officer, we had hired more than forty new faculty members, and we had never had a conversation in the community about that core value and curricular requirement. Having heard many complaints about the Bible requirement among arts and science faculty, I knew that I had failed to address this erosion in our core values.

I met with the faculty who taught the undergraduate Bible curriculum and explained the situation. I asked them if they would do two things—first, discuss and articulate together the content and rationale for the curriculum in its current state, and then, in the next academic year present that curriculum as a proposal to the whole faculty, which we would then discuss in four open faculty meetings, revise, and finally approve collectively. The Bible faculty at first complained that they did not have time for such a long process and expressed their fears that the wider faculty might not reaffirm the existing requirement. I insisted that this was a risk we had to take. If the full faculty did not support this as a core component of our mission, then we would have failed in our responsibility to demonstrate its central value. The process demanded even more work than the faculty had anticipated, but in the end, they made significant improvements in the curriculum, and the wider faculty endorsed the revised program as a core component of Biola's undergraduate education.

At Fuller Theological Seminary we have faced similar challenges, and the president and the faculty engage annually in conversations that focus on the core values and mission of the seminary. A few years ago the faculty became deeply concerned about the distortions they heard from students about the essence of the gospel of Jesus Christ. In the academic year 2003–4, the faculty held a yearlong conversation around the question, what is the gospel? The next year the same faculty members each prepared a message for seminary chapel on the same theme. Renewal must be intentional, it must become part of our regular work, and it must continue over a substantive period of time.

"Body" Work—The Hope of Leadership

The essence of effective leading for multicultural teams may be summed up in the phrase "body work," or "being disciples to make disciples." We cannot expect to be effective in the ministry of the kingdom of God if we are not following Christ. We must begin by being disciples if we hope to be able to make disciples and make a difference in our world. Again, as we reflect on the teams in the case studies we have discussed, the conflicts within them all are the result of a failure to obey Christ in relationships with one another. None of these teams had a commitment to covenant community. Team leaders did not focus on covenant community as a key component of the work of the team.

"Body work" is always messy—good, bad, beautiful, ugly. The members of D-Team (chapter 7) divided over their values for hierarchy and equity. Tawat clung so tenaciously to his values for hierarchy that his egalitarian team members refused to work with him. Brian, the leader, was so frustrated that he at times did not even consult his team, and this proved to be his undoing. Yet Brian and leaders like him are not without hope. Although the process of confronting one another in prayerful love is painful, when we commit to pray, seeking the direction of the Holy Spirit, and then confront in Jesus's way, God works on our behalf. Unity is the result of intense testing and struggle, in which people experience first the acceptance and love of the leader and then learn to accept and love one another in spite of their differences.

Tawat was absolutely a challenge for Brian; would he ever relinquish even a small part of his hierarchical identity to meet his egalitarian teammates in unity? Brian and Tawat must begin with a conversation about being the body of Christ and loving one another within that body. They need to explore together what that means and how we cannot hope to do the work of the kingdom unless we obey Christ in this matter. Brian and Tawat must talk together about hierarchy and equity and explore how their common identity in Christ might minimize these conflicts.

If we examine the other multicultural teams in Lorraine Dierck's (2007) study in Thailand (chapter 7), we see that they all faced inherent conflicts of hierarchical values versus egalitarian values among their teams' members. One of those teams (C) adopted the corporate hierarchy social game, framed around Thai values and expectations, and worked effectively together. Another team (E) adopted the egalitarian philosophy of their expatriate members, and, with some adjustments in consideration of their Thai members, they worked effectively together. Each of these teams listened to their members, and after some discussion and adjustments over time, they agreed to a structure and values that served their members and the work of the ministry. However, four of the teams in Dierck's study failed to reach a compromise, and although they carried on their work, they struggled, like Brian and Tawat, with conflicting values and division among team members.

Brian must place his hope in the work of the Holy Spirit and the power of the Word of God to speak to him and his teammates. Brian does not have the power to change the minds of any of his team members—but he does have the authority to pray for them, and with them, and then to engage them around the issues of uniting together as the people of God on the mission of God. They need to dialogue together about the pain of disunity and the frustration they all have experienced in the long meetings that have led to separation and discord. They need to discuss their differences about social structure, values, and decision making and continue asking how they might find a common ground for ministry.

In the end the work of the kingdom depends on our obedience to the King. God cannot rule in people who are disobedient and in conflict with one another. God rules as we obey God and love one another. As a leader, Brian must commit his energy to obeying the command to love God and to love his team members as himself; in so doing he will have begun the work essential to building an effective multicultural team. While the process will be difficult, with periods of intense testing and struggle, building covenant community is a process of refocusing *from* doing what we want *to* being the people of God.

The Cross—The Defining Metaphor of Leadership

David Bennett's book *Metaphors of Ministry* (1993) notes that the writers of the Gospels and the Epistles in the New Testament rarely use the "rule over" words and metaphors that are a part of Greek New Testament culture and common in our own society today. As we think about leading cross-culturally, we employ many metaphors in our organizations that promote the "rule over" relationships engrained in our societies. Missions have CEOs, field directors, or superintendents. Teams have team directors or team leaders. Functional hierarchies are very often defined in the leadership structures of teams. This vocabulary and these metaphors are embedded in the social games (chapters 3, 4, and 5) and worldviews that structure our relationships in life and community.

As we reflect on the kind of leadership essential for leading multicultural teams, Bennett helps us to refocus our thinking *away from* the "rule over" metaphors that pervade our cultural life and work *toward* the metaphors used by Jesus and the apostles as reported by the writers of the Gospels and the Epistles in the New Testament. I suggest that in this context the cross is the defining metaphor for leadership given by the Lord Jesus Christ.

Jesus said, "Those who would be my disciples must deny themselves and take up their cross daily and follow me. For those who want to save their life will lose it, but those who lose their life for me will save it" (Luke 9:23–24). How does the metaphor "to take up their cross daily" define the practice of leadership? As we consider covenant community and empowering others as discussed in this book, we recognize that we cannot accomplish the work of the kingdom of God by using the power structures of our society and our culture and by seeking our own fulfillment and recognition. This is precisely the conversation that must happen in the D-Teams, divided and discontented, in Thailand. The people on these teams, who have blocked consensus on structure, values, and unity, must come together at the cross. Whatever their disagreements, the message of the cross is "lose your life for my sake." The challenge for leaders and members alike is to relinquish those positions that seem precious, to listen to one another, and then in the presence and power of the Holy Spirit, to find the place of unity where they can move forward together.

Our work is intended to fulfill the kingdom vision that Jesus brought to his disciples and to proclaim to a broken world that the kingdom of God is at hand. Jesus makes it very clear that to accomplish that vision we must take up the cross—through sacrificing our quest for power, our emotional needs for acceptance and recognition, our obsession to have "my will" implemented—thereby denying ourselves and following him. Pastor David discovered the power of this truth when he listened to the women elders in his congregation and in fear and trembling agreed to their request to change his plan for their prayer retreat. By surrendering his will, he opened the channels of trust and communication with his elders, and that act transformed his ministry.

As a power-giving leader, I must begin at the cross. As members of multicultural teams and as leaders of multicultural teams, we all together must begin at the cross. Jesus's death on the cross is the metaphor repeated over and over again in the New Testament. Peter reminds us that Jesus left us an example that we "should follow in his steps" (1 Pet. 2:21). As he spells out the details of that example, we see Jesus tolerating insults and abuse and not retaliating in any way (v. 23). We see him suffering, being threatened, and not threatening in return. We see him going to the cross and giving up his life on our behalf without rebuke or recrimination.

Marta, middle manager of the literacy and translation team, and Brian, from D-Team in Thailand, have each faced team opposition that has paralyzed their ministries. Bizu criticized Marta, misused materials, took pay without work, and generally undermined Marta's leadership and credibility. Tawat challenged Brian's wisdom, judged him naive, and undermined his decisions. What would it mean for Marta and Brian to go with their teammates to the cross? Peter notes that Jesus tolerated insults and abuse and did not retaliate in any way. This is the first change that Marta and Brian could make. Each had retaliated in specific ways against their colleagues. Marta in particular was hurt, and in her pain she acted against Bizu on several occasions. The second change they could make is to sacrifice themselves, or some significant aspect of their ministry, for their brothers. Marta may have more opportunity to do this than Brian, as Bizu is clearly a needy person, struggling both economically and spiritually. Brian may need to find some way to show Tawat how much he is willing to sacrifice on his behalf. Neither Tawat nor Bizu seems to understand the scope of the cross and the profound significance of the work of Jesus in their lives.

Worship at the Cross—Motivation for Change

"Taking up the cross" is an act of worship. We fall on our face at the foot of the cross, confess our sin and shame, and express our gratitude for the unfathomable grace of God's acceptance and forgiveness. In worship we submit our will to God and relinquish our quest for power and control and our need to ensure the outcomes that we want so desperately to achieve as leaders of multicultural teams. We acknowledge our powerlessness, that we cannot change one person or effect one ministry achievement apart from the grace of God. In worship we ask the Holy Spirit to replace these old obsessions with a new obsession to obey Jesus Christ.

Leaders in particular must surrender their obsession to control and achieve, through worship at the cross. Of all the cases we have considered, Marcus (chapter 11) struggled most obviously with an obsession to control. He overruled his teammates, insisted that things be done in his way, and embarrassed his coworker Sarah to the point that she dreaded reporting to the donor for their project. If Marcus were willing to go humbly to the cross, relinquish his power, and honor and love his teammates, God would transform the team and this ministry through the power of his grace.

The act of worship at the cross and surrender to the Holy Spirit enables us to release the control of our lives, teams, and work into the hands of God. We discover freedom through faith to be about the work of the kingdom of God. When we insist on reasserting our control, of managing the outcomes to accomplish what we believe God wants, we have stepped away from the cross and moved back into a position where we see ourselves as king instead of worshiping and following the King of kings and the Lord of lords.

When we worship and live in obedience to the King of kings, God transforms leaders, teams, and every form of social game into covenant communities, called out for the mission of God and working together in unity to fulfill their divine purpose. When we worship at the cross, we learn to take the path of weakness rather than of power, to extend mutual forgiveness rather than condemnation, and to submit to one another rather than seeking power and the subjection of others to our will in our relationships and teamwork.

References

Adams, Richard N. 1975. *Energy and Structure: A Theory of Social Power*. Austin: University of Texas.

Banks, Robert J., and Bernice M. Ledbetter. 2004. *Reviewing Leadership: A Christian Evaluation of Current Approaches*. Grand Rapids: Baker Academic.

Barth, Markus, and Helmut Blanke. 2000. *The Letter to Philemon: A New Translation with Notes and Commentary*. Grand Rapids: Eerdmans.

Bennett, David W. 1993. *Metaphors of Ministry*. Grand Rapids: Baker Academic.

Christian, Jayakumar. 1994. "Powerlessness of the Poor: Toward an Alternative Kingdom of God Based Paradigm for Response." PhD diss., Fuller Theological Seminary, Pasadena, CA.

Collins, Jim, and Jerry I. Porras. 1994. *Built to Last: Successful Habits of Visionary Companies*. New York: HarperCollins.

DePree, Max. 2004. *Leadership Is an Art*. New York: Currency.

Dierck, Lorraine W. 2007. "Teams That Work: Leadership, Power, and Decision-Making in Multicultural Teams in Thailand." DMiss diss., Biola University, La Mirada, CA.

Dorff, Elliot N. 2006. "Jewish Models of Leadership." In Mouw and Jacobsen, *Traditions in Leadership*, 4–40.

Douglas, Mary. 1982. "Cultural Bias." In *In the Active Voice*, 183–254. London: Routledge & Kegan Paul.

Flanders, Christopher L. 2005. "About Face: Reorienting Thai Face for Soteriology and Mission." PhD diss., Fuller Theological Seminary, Pasadena, CA.

Guder, Darrell L. 2000. *The Continuing Conversion of the Church*. Grand Rapids: Eerdmans.

Gupta, Paul R., and Sherwood G. Lingenfelter. 2006. *Breaking Tradition to Accomplish Vision: Training Leaders for a Church-Planting Movement; A Case from India*. Winona Lake, IN: BMH Books.

Hesselgrave, David J. 2005. *Paradigms in Conflict: 10 Key Questions in Christian Missions Today*. Grand Rapids: Kregel.

Hofstede, Geert. 2001. *Culture's Consequences: Comparing Values, Behaviors, Institutions and Organizations across Nations*. 2nd ed. Thousand Oaks, CA: Sage.

Koeshall, Anita. 2008. "Toward a Theory of Dynamic Asymmetry and Redeemed Power—A Case Study of Reflexive Agents in German Pentecostal Churches." PhD diss., Fuller Theological Seminary, Pasadena, CA.

Lingenfelter, Sherwood. 1996. *Agents of Transformation*. Grand Rapids: Baker Academic.

———. 1998. *Transforming Culture*. Grand Rapids: Baker Academic.

Lingenfelter, Sherwood G., and Marvin K. Mayers. 2003. *Ministering Cross-Culturally*. 2nd ed. Grand Rapids: Baker Academic.

Linthicum, Robert. 2003. *Transforming Power: Biblical Strategies for Making a Difference in Your Community*. Downers Grove, IL: InterVarsity.

Lohfink, Gerhard. 1984. *Jesus and Community: The Social Dimensions of the Christian Faith*. Translated by John P. Galvin. Philadelphia: Fortress.

Mouw, Richard J. 2006. "Leadership and the Three-Fold Office of Christ." In Mouw and Jacobsen, *Traditions in Leadership*, 118–38.

Mouw, Richard J., and Eric O. Jacobsen, eds. 2006. *Traditions in Leadership: How Faith Traditions Shape the Way We Lead*. Pasadena, CA: DePree Leadership Center.

Myers, Bryant L. 2002. *Walking with the Poor: Principles and Practices of Transformational Development*. Maryknoll, NY: Orbis.

Shuster, Marguerite. 1987. *Power, Pathology, Paradox: The Dynamics of Evil and Good*. Grand Rapids: Zondervan.

Stackhouse, Max L. 1997. *Covenant and Commitments: Faith, Family, and Economic Life*. Louisville: Westminster John Knox.

Steffen, Tom. 1997. *Passing the Baton: Church Planting That Empowers*. La Habra, CA: Center for Organizational & Ministry Development.

Watson, David. 1978. *I Believe in the Church*. Grand Rapids: Eerdmans.

Watters, John. 2007. "Lessons Learned from Wycliffe's Journey into Cross-Cultural Partnerships." Presentation given at the Coalition on the Support of Indigenous Missionaries Conference, June 11–13, 2007, Wheaton College, and written personal communications prepared for this manuscript.

Weaver, Alan Ray. 2004. "Toward a Cross-Cultural Theory of Leadership Emergence: The Hungarian Case." PhD diss., Fuller Theological Seminary, Pasadena, CA.

Willard, Dallas. 1998. *The Divine Conspiracy: Rediscovering Our Hidden Life in God*. San Francisco: Harper.

Wood, Richard J. 2006. "Christ Has Come to Teach His People Himself: Vulnerability and the Exercise of Power in Quaker Leadership." In Mouw and Jacobsen, *Traditions in Leadership*, 208–21.

Wright, Tom. 2004. *Paul for Everyone: The Prison Letters; Ephesians, Philippians, Colossians, Philemon*. Louisville: Westminster John Knox.

Wright, Walter C., Jr. 2000. *Relational Leadership: A Biblical Model for Leadership and Service*. Waynesboro, GA: Paternoster.

Yamamori, Tetsunao. 1993. *Penetrating Mission's Final Frontier: A New Strategy for Unreached Peoples*. Downers Grove, IL: InterVarsity.

Yancey, Philip. 1997. *What's So Amazing about Grace?* Grand Rapids: Zondervan.

Index